YESTERDAY THE CHILDREN
WERE DANCING

Inquiries about the production of this play
in English should be addressed to the publishers,
Clarke, Irwin & Company Limited
791 St. Clair Avenue West, Toronto, Ont.

By the same author
Bousille and the Just
Tit-Coq

YESTERDAY
THE CHILDREN
WERE DANCING

GRATIEN GÉLINAS

Translated from the French by
Mavor Moore

CLARKE, IRWIN & COMPANY LIMITED

Toronto, Vancouver

© Canada, 1967
by Clarke, Irwin & Company Limited

ISBN 0 7720 0210 x

7 8 9 10 JD 79 78 77 76 75 74 73 72

Printed in Canada

The premiere performance in English of *Yesterday the Children Were Dancing* was given by the Charlottetown Festival in Prince Edward Island, on July 5, 1967 with the following cast:

PIERRE GRAVEL *a lawyer*	Gratien Gélinas
PAUL O'BRIEN *Gravel's brother-in-law and partner*	Jacques Auger
RAOUL ROBERGE *a political organizer*	Yvon Dufour
LARRY GRAVEL *Gravel's younger son*	Pascal Gélinas
BERTHE MARTIN *a secretary*	Anne Collings
NICOLE CHARTIER *a university student*	Suzanne Levesque
ANDRÉ GRAVEL *Gravel's elder son*	Yves Gélinas
LOUISE GRAVEL *Pierre Gravel's wife*	Huguette Oligny

Directed by Gratien Gélinas and Mavor Moore

Set by Jean-Claude Rinfret

Costume design by Marie Day

Properties by Kent Sloan

The action of the play unfolds without interruption. As a courtesy to the audience, however, the curtain falls at the end of Scene Five. When it rises again after Intermission, the characters are found in exactly the same situation in which we left them.

YESTERDAY THE CHILDREN
WERE DANCING

ACT ONE

SCENE ONE

The Gravel's living-room in Montreal. The Present.

The atmosphere is one of elegance and more especially of warmth. The furniture is in good taste, but one feels that a woman of serenity has chosen it less to impress visitors than to assure the relaxation of family and friends. The sofa and chairs are, above all, comfortable. One leaves them regretfully, the way one also leaves the room itself. In the left wall is a fireplace and on the back wall, a bookcase contains a record-player and a discreet liquor-cabinet. In the centre a small vestibule opens onto the unseen part of the ground floor and onto the stairway, which leads to the second floor. On the right wall, a picture-window gives onto the street, which is hidden by curtains and drapes. Behind the sofa, which occupies the centre of the room, a narrow table holds the telephone. A sewing basket, a green plant, some newspapers and magazines—and maybe a set of chessmen somewhere— complete the lived-in atmosphere of the room without cluttering it.

When the curtain rises, O'BRIEN *is alone on stage: he is sitting in an easy chair, reading a newspaper. On a small table nearby sits a glass of cognac. In a moment,* GRAVEL *enters.*

GRAVEL, *seeing him:*   Ah! You got in all right! [*He sets down a small briefcase.*]

3

O'BRIEN: As you see.

GRAVEL, *taking off his overcoat and hanging it in the vestibule*:   I was afraid you might have been kept waiting outside.

O'BRIEN: I rang, and Larry let me in.

GRAVEL: Good. Is he still here?

O'BRIEN: Went up to his room, I think.

GRAVEL: Been waiting long?

O'BRIEN: Five minutes, that's all. [*Indicating the paper*] Just gave me time to catch up on the world. You read about that separatist incident last night in Quebec?

GRAVEL: The bomb, you mean? Listen, that's small beer compared with my news.

O'BRIEN: You have a bomb, too, eh!

GRAVEL: Wait till you hear! Do you know Raoul Roberge?

O'BRIEN, *searching his memory*:   Roberge. . .

GRAVEL: The local Liberal organizer.

O'BRIEN: I doubt it.

GRAVEL: He's just parking his car. Pretend you know him: it'll make introductions easier.

O'BRIEN: I get it.

GRAVEL: I'm sorry to rout you out, but I really had to see you.

O'BRIEN: It's perfectly all right. I'm at your service.

GRAVEL: Paul, I find myself in a fantastic situation.

O'BRIEN: Good or bad?

GRAVEL, *with ill-concealed enthusiasm*:   I wish I knew! I called you in to help me make up my mind, especially as it involves you, in a way.

O'BRIEN: Well, if I can do anything.

GRAVEL: You get up one fine Sunday morning, all serene, at peace with yourself, no suspicion that come nightfall, wham! you're at a crossroads in your life.

4

O'BRIEN: As serious as that?

GRAVEL: Paul, it's all very simple: I've just been knocked for a loop!

The doorbell rings during the preceding speech and ROBERGE *appears.*

ROBERGE, to GRAVEL: Hey! Better lock your door—reporters on our tail.

GRAVEL: Never mind the reporters—let me have your things. [Introducing O'BRIEN] Paul O'Brien, my wife's brother . . . and my partner for twenty-four years. You get the connection?—with your proposition, I mean.

O'BRIEN: Good evening, Roberge. Do I gather you two are cooking up some nefarious plot?

ROBERGE: Not at all! But all afternoon he's been moaning: "What'll Paul think of this business?" I have news for you: your dear brother-in-law and partner is scared stiff of you.

O'BRIEN: He is? He's a better fencer!

ROBERGE: Maybe, but you're a better lawyer. That's why you'll get along fine without him. You'll never know the difference. Meanwhile I take him off your hands and make him a star—in politics.

GRAVEL: Hear that? It'll give you an idea of what I've been put through today.

ROBERGE: And I'm not talking about small-time provincial stuff: I'm talking about the big-time—Ottawa.

GRAVEL: Never mind the sales pitch. Phone the committee: there may be some news.

ROBERGE: I'll do anything you want, if you'll give me a drink!

GRAVEL: What would you like?

ROBERGE, *heading for the phone*:   Scotch.

GRAVEL, *producing the bottles and glasses*:   Water? Ice?

ROBERGE: Straight. And make it a double. If I ever needed a pick-me-up, today's the day. [*Dials the number*]

GRAVEL: Paul, what can I give you?

O'BRIEN: Not a thing. [*Indicating his glass*] I took the liberty of helping myself to a brandy while I was waiting.

GRAVEL: Right. A brandy will stand you in good stead when you hear the whole story.

ROBERGE, *on the phone*:   Hello? . . . Roberge. Any word from the hospital? . . . No change, uh! . . . I'm at Gravel's house. Let me know the minute there's something new.

GRAVEL, *handing him his drink*:   Give them the number: it's not in the book.

ROBERGE, *reading the number from the phone*:   Write this down: 842-4639. It's an unlisted number: if you give it to a reporter I'll skin you alive. . . . What?

GRAVEL, *pouring himself a glass of mineral water*:   I think I'll stick to water. Keep a clear head: I'm going to need one.

ROBERGE, *on the phone*:   Right. [*Hangs up. To* GRAVEL] He's still in a coma.

GRAVEL: Poor fellow.

ROBERGE: Before it slips my mind, your wife just called the committee rooms. Seems you'd promised to call her at St. Marc sometime this afternoon.

GRAVEL: I didn't forget. I just hadn't the courage.

ROBERGE: Pierre, you're making a mountain out of a molehill.

GRAVEL: Anyway, I'll have to send someone to get her.

ROBERGE: If I were in your shoes, I'd make up my own mind, like a man.

GRAVEL, *calling from the foot of the stairs*: Larry!

ROBERGE: With women, you're smarter to do first and explain later.

GRAVEL: Sorry, but I've always taken the sharp curves holding my wife's hand.

LARRY, *appearing on the stairway*: Calling me?

GRAVEL: Come down for a second. [*Introducing him to* ROBERGE] My younger son, Larry. Irish stock, but well assimilated—like his uncle-godfather, there.

ROBERGE: Glad to know you, Larry.

LARRY, *greeting him vaguely*: Sir . . .

ROBERGE, *to* LARRY, *kidding*: I hope you're not one of those young jerks who heckled Pearson at the Show Mart last Thursday. . . .

LARRY: I got better things to do.

ROBERGE: That's the stuff. Save your steam for the Diefenbaker meeting Tuesday.

GRAVEL: Larry, is your brother up there?

LARRY: No, but he'll be back anytime: he wants to see you.

GRAVEL: Fine—I'll be around.

ROBERGE: Kids!—always got a hand out for more dough!

GRAVEL, *as* LARRY *starts to go back upstairs*: Wait a second: your mother has to be picked up.

LARRY: In St. Marc?

GRAVEL: It's five past seven: you can make it back by eight-twenty, without speeding. [*As* LARRY *hesitates*] Look: I know it's tough on you, on a lovely Sunday . . . [*Giving him the car keys*] but keep the car for the rest of the evening if you like—maybe take out a girl.

LARRY, *taking the keys*: Okay. [*He starts upstairs.*]

GRAVEL: I'll do the same for you sometime.

LARRY, *before disappearing upstairs*:   Say, did you ask
your secretary to come over and type something?

GRAVEL: Yes: my speech. Why?

LARRY: She phoned to say she'll be here a little after
seven.

GRAVEL: Thanks.

LARRY *vanishes upstairs.*

O'BRIEN: Listen, you may get a kick out of keeping me
on tenterhooks, but I'd like to know what's up, if nobody minds.

ROBERGE: You're in the dark about all this, eh?

O'BRIEN: I may look as if I'd just stepped out of Limbo,
but I've spent the afternoon closeted in the office,
drawing up a deed.

ROBERGE: Ah, that's the way to spend Sunday in Montreal!

LARRY *comes down, ready to go.*

GRAVEL, *to* LARRY: Better get the tank filled: you'll
need it.

LARRY: Okay. [*He goes out.*]

O'BRIEN: There was no one on the switchboard, so it
wasn't until I called home I learned Pierre wanted
me here as soon as I could make it.

GRAVEL: Well! Here's the picture, Paul. At eleven-
thirty this morning, Arthur Duranceau collapsed on
the sidewalk in front of his house. A brain hemorrhage—a dandy!

O'BRIEN: Duranceau? . . . The Minister of Justice?

ROBERGE: The same. Lying half-dead since noon,
under an oxygen tent at the Hôtel-Dieu. With a
general election two weeks from tomorrow!

O'BRIEN: His first attack?

8

ROBERGE: Second . . . second-and-a-half. He didn't brag about it, naturally.

O'BRIEN: I saw him on television Friday night: he looked fine.

GRAVEL: I'll go you one better: he was at the hockey game last night. We left the Forum together as usual. He said, "Could you sub for me at Sorel tomorrow afternoon? I promised Ferland I'd address his meeting, but I'm feeling lazy." I told him: "I'd be happy to, my dear fellow, but I'm leaving right away for St. Marc with my wife, to try and finish up a talk I have to give Monday at the Canadian Club in Toronto. But call me about one o'clock," I said, "and if it looks as if I'll get through in time, I'll be there." Then just as we got to his car, his chauffeur said to him: "I have some news for you: the radio just announced that a terrorist bomb toppled the new Wolfe monument in Quebec City about an hour ago. . . ." Well sir, his face fell a mile. He muttered grimly, "Forget it, my friend: that settles it. No Minister of Justice can duck this issue: I'll have to tackle it tomorrow, myself."

ROBERGE: That's not his headache; it's the Province's.

GRAVEL: So I went to St. Marc, and got up at five this morning. I was still hard at work when the phone rang just before noon. It was him [*Indicating* ROBERGE] all het up.

ROBERGE: I said, "Get here as quick as you can. We've got to call a council meeting: Duranceau has just been taken to hospital."

GRAVEL: So off I dash, leaving a note for Louise, who was away off somewhere on the mountain, gathering autumn leaves. I get to the Windsor. I find them all running round in circles like chicks without a hen.

9

ROBERGE: Ever since, we've been tearing our hair out together.

O'BRIEN *to* ROBERGE: Just great for you, eh?

ROBERGE: I've been an organizer for seventeen years, but I want to tell you I've never been in a box like this.

GRAVEL: If he stays alive till polling-day, there's no problem: his wife can get out and campaign for him.

ROBERGE: We had a thirteen thousand majority in '63. It's in the bag!

GRAVEL: But if the party doesn't put up anyone else before two o'clock tomorrow—the deadline for nomination, remember—and if he actually dies before election day, then we're really up the creek.

ROBERGE: The riding's voted Liberal for years, but no candidate, no seat—it's as simple as that.

O'BRIEN: There's some consolation, though: think how happy this could make the poor N.D.P.!

ROBERGE, *growling*: To hell with the N.D.P.!

GRAVEL, *to* O'BRIEN: Watch it—he'll have a hemorrhage too!

ROBERGE: No, my friend, there's no other way. The party has to come up with another candidate before two o'clock tomorrow. And besides, you can always withdraw at the last minute if by some miracle Duranceau pulls through till the election.

GRAVEL, *to* O'BRIEN: You see what he's leading up to?

O'BRIEN: I begin to deduce the motive of the crime.

GRAVEL: They've been twisting my arm since two this afternoon.

ROBERGE: Why not! You're the only one who can get us out of this!

GRAVEL, *scoffing*: I am, eh?

ROBERGE: Look: she didn't know it at the time, but your mother brought you into the world for this!

10

GRAVEL: Anybody can take that riding. You just said it's in the bag. And you can bet Fournier's itching to jump into the firing-line. Give him the high sign and he'll turn out at six tomorrow morning, loaded for bear, at the door of the Returning Officer, deposit at the ready!

ROBERGE: That's not the point—"Will he or won't he!" —The point is, who needs him? We'd have to make do with Fournier if you weren't around: but who wants him!

GRAVEL: He's nobody's fool.

ROBERGE: No, but he's a softie, a jelly-fish. Fournier talks big, but he's a yes-man, and Parliament's full of yes-men up to here; Pearson's always saying it. What we really need is a strong government—not just in numbers but in quality: men with guts who know what they're doing and won't go round licking the Separatists' boots. If every man who could stand up to them stays in his warm bed making love to his wife, what the hell's going to happen to the country?

GRAVEL: Since I've already heard that argument three times today, I think I'll go and call my wife. [*He goes to the phone and dials.*]

ROBERGE, *picking up the paper which* O'BRIEN *was reading at curtain-rise*: You know, I really thought we'd seen the last of that nonsense: I really did.

O'BRIEN: I guess not.

ROBERGE: But the provincial police are onto these terrorists pretty fast—don't let the grass grow under their feet.

O'BRIEN: This time, they won't have to look far: the culprit's already behind bars.

ROBERGE: Well whaddya know!

O'BRIEN: The kid gave himself up half an hour after it happened.

11

GRAVEL, *to himself, on the phone*: How come she doesn't answer?

ROBERGE: He gave himself up? You mean it?

O'BRIEN: A crime confessed is half a pardon.

ROBERGE: You know, it takes a college boy to come up with a screwy idea like that.

O'BRIEN: This time it was a twenty-two-year-old worker, from the Lower Town.

ROBERGE: Another damn Union fanatic, eh!

O'BRIEN: Poor old Wolfe! Poor old monument! Didn't have a chance!

ROBERGE: Don't expect me to shed the first tear.

GRAVEL, *on the phone*: Hello? Louise? . . . Did you find my note on the table? . . . Yes: he's still in a coma. I'm sorry to call you so late, but I got caught up in a terrible tangle, and . . . Darling, what's happening to me is like a fairy-tale or a nightmare, or maybe both. Anyway, it's not something we can discuss on the phone; I'd rather wait till I see you. Larry's on his way to pick you up. Your brother's here. We'll have a family council, and . . . What? . . . Hold it a minute. [*To the others*] Sauriol from Le Devoir just called St. Marc and asked her to confirm or deny the rumour that I'm going to replace Duranceau tomorrow.

ROBERGE, *jumping up*: Damn it to hell!

GRAVEL, *on the phone*: You said you didn't know a thing, I hope? . . . Good girl!

ROBERGE, *relieved*: She'll make a wonderful wife for a cabinet minister!

GRAVEL, *on the phone*: Well, I'm glad, you know more about it than I thought you did. . . . No, no: save your comments till you get here, but think about it on the way. I have to make up my mind tonight. . . . Right: it's that stupid. I'll be waiting, darling. . . . Bye now.

ROBERGE, *as* GRAVEL *starts to hang up*: Hey, let me speak to her for a second.

GRAVEL, *hanging up*: Now look: no high-pressuring. She's my wife and I'll do the persuading.

ROBERGE: Sure: only—

GRAVEL: Listen: I warned you when you insisted on coming with me: I need to think this out with my family. So get set to make yourself scarce and let me think. With you around it's impossible.

ROBERGE: Bloody perfectionist, that's what you are! Quit shivering in your shoes and—

GRAVEL, *indicating* O'BRIEN: I can't just drop him like a cigar butt and skip off to Ottawa, can I?

The telephone rings.

ROBERGE, *beating* GRAVEL *to the phone*: Let me get it—it may be La Presse this time.

GRAVEL: Simmer down: I told you it's an unlisted number.

ROBERGE: You never know. [*Answering*] Hello? . . . Just a moment, please. [*His hand over the mouth-piece*] The dulcet voice of a novice angel wants to talk to André.

GRAVEL: Must be his girl friend. [*Takes the phone*] Hello? . . . I'm sorry, Nicole, André is out. But his brother tells me he'll likely be back later. Will I get him to call you?

ROBERGE: Oh to be in love instead of politics—especially on a Sunday night!

GRAVEL, *at the phone, scribbling on a pad*: A Social Science textbook, with a red binding. Who's the author, again? . . . Fine: I'll go and have a look in his room as soon as I can. Good-night, my dear. [*Hangs up*]

ROBERGE, *to* O'BRIEN: You want to know, in two words,

what's biting this guy? For twenty years he's been itching to get active in politics and now he has the chance he hasn't the guts to take it.

GRAVEL: That's just it: look before you leap, my friend. I got cured of blind dates long ago, after that little binge with the Bloc Populaire in '44.

ROBERGE: That'll teach you to renounce the true faith —Liberal, that is.

GRAVEL: I came out of it looking like a first-class fool and up to my ears in debt. [*Indicating* O'BRIEN] Thank God he was there, keeping the home fires burning, or I'd have been in a bad way. Married only a year, André a babe in arms . . .

ROBERGE: A youthful indiscretion, that's all that was. We all make mistakes. You came back to the fold like the prodigal son and today we're killing the fatted calf in your honour—a little belated maybe, but better late than never. As a matter of fact, we'd 've gladly slit its throat ages ago if you'd agreed to be our candidate in '57, or any election since!

GRAVEL: But what was I supposed to do: turn hand-springs? The only thing I know is the Law. There was Duranceau, a good friend of mine, firmly settled in the Justice Ministry. I wasn't going to start messing around with Agriculture or Fisheries. What do I know about them! Not a bloody thing!

ROBERGE, *a mutter*: You wouldn't have been the first.

GRAVEL: As for giving up sixty thousand a year to sit in the back benches and rot away. . . . No, thank you very much!

ROBERGE: Okay, but now the post is vacant.

GRAVEL: Just a minute: Duranceau is still alive.

ROBERGE: Come off it! You know as well as I do he's done for. Have a little faith in your stars!

GRAVEL, *to* O'BRIEN: The gall of the man!

ROBERGE: I'll tell you this: whether you like it or not, the Minister of Justice is no longer, his chair is empty. It's yours for the asking.

GRAVEL: And I'll tell you this: you're in a tight spot. Promise her anything, but give her Arpège—isn't that about it?

ROBERGE: When I make a promise I keep it. I'm not a candidate, I'm an organizer.

GRAVEL: You can get me elected like that [*Snaps fingers*]—I know: I've seen your machine in action.

ROBERGE: With you I don't need a machine.

GRAVEL: But choosing a cabinet is the prerogative of the Prime Minister, not you.

ROBERGE: It so happens Pearson and I are on the same wave-length nine times out of ten. And the tenth time, he's the one who goofs.

GRAVEL: What about Delage?

ROBERGE: Relax: Delage will stay on in the Privy Council. Pearson would never toss him back among the lions.

GRAVEL: Then Archambault? You think he'll sit on his backside while a greenhorn noses past him?

ROBERGE: I'll fill you in on that, confidentially of course. Archambault's all set to be Chief Justice of the Supreme Court. It's been written in the Liberal sky ever since McNaughton bowed out last spring. Anyway, he's too old for anything else.

GRAVEL: You know, even if I were tempted to take you at your word, he [*Indicating* O'BRIEN] mightn't be so easily persuaded. I know him too well: he never says much, but his mind works away. The moment your back's turned, he'll ask for written proof: he's a good lawyer.

ROBERGE: You want proof? Okay, you'll have it—in no

15

time. If you have to have proof before you'll believe, proof you'll get—Doubting Thomas!

The doorbell rings.

GRAVEL, *to* O'BRIEN: Would you mind seeing who it is?

SCENE TWO

The SECRETARY *enters.*

SECRETARY: I let myself in: that's all right?

GRAVEL: Perfectly.

SECRETARY: Evening, Mr. O'Brien.

GRAVEL, *to* ROBERGE: You know my secretary, Miss Martin?

ROBERGE: And I hope to know her better!

GRAVEL: Sorry to bring you out so late.

SECRETARY: I don't mind.

GRAVEL: I intended to let you have the speech early in the afternoon, but the damnedest things have been happening to me.

SECRETARY: Yes, I know.

GRAVEL: You do?

SECRETARY: Just as I was leaving the house, the radio news carried some rumours about you.

O'BRIEN: Quite right. Your boss got up this morning like a good boy, but before the day is out he may take a turn for the worse.

SECRETARY: Congratulations; it sounds exciting!

GRAVEL: Nerve-wracking might be more like it!

ROBERGE: Incidentally, ma'am, while you're at it you might dig up his latest *curriculum vitae*.

GRAVEL: Now wait: I've got more important things for her to do right now. [*Passing a manuscript to the*

16

SECRETARY] Here's the rest of what I gave you Friday.

SECRETARY: The first part's already done: I mimeographed twenty-five copies.

GRAVEL: Do you remember how many pages so far?

SECRETARY: Seventeen.

GRAVEL: That should be good for forty minutes.

SECRETARY: Would you like a draft first?

GRAVEL: No thanks, there's not enough time. But maybe you should read it through in my study in case there is something you don't understand.

SECRETARY: Fine.

GRAVEL: Then you can type it all out. And do me the usual favour: correct any mistakes.

SECRETARY: This is the whole thing?

GRAVEL: Still two or three paragraphs to come at the end. I'd got that far this morning when the phone rang and the earthquake started. But I'll try to think up a grand finale on the plane tomorrow.

The SECRETARY *exits toward* GRAVEL'S *study.*

ROBERGE: If you want to end with a bang, tell them you're running for Parliament; that'll make headlines.

GRAVEL: Won't give up, eh? [*To* O'BRIEN] He's like a puppy to a root!

ROBERGE: And you can tell them the Liberal Party is the only party that can give the country—

GRAVEL: Listen: I'm giving a talk on political affairs, but it's strictly non-partisan—a talk I took on six months ago. How was I to know it'd come smack in the middle of a campaign!

ROBERGE: A good disciple should never miss a chance to preach the gospel according to Lester B. Pearson.

GRAVEL: Wait a minute: I've just thought of something. That damn talk, you know, presents a serious complication.

ROBERGE: How's that?

GRAVEL: I can't be in two places at once, flying to Toronto and registering in Montreal. I'd have to cancel the speech, and that would be disastrous. The Canadian Club in Toronto is no joke.

ROBERGE: Go, man, go! What's the problem? Sign the slip, that's all, and leave the rest to me. As I told you, the organizer is more important than the candidate.

GRAVEL: Just like that? You think I could?

ROBERGE: It's cut and dried! What time's your flight?

GRAVEL: I'm confirmed for nine, on the waiting list for ten-thirty.

ROBERGE: Nothing to it! We'll get you onto that second plane if we have to kill someone else. At nine-o-five I'll take you to the Windsor for your press conference. By nine-twenty you're out of there, duly photographed for the papers and TV. I rush you to Dorval with a police escort by ten-fifteen. By twelve-thirty you're in downtown Toronto, speech in hand. Meantime, I'll get you coverage like you've never seen!— Canadian Press, Time Magazine—at today's prices, fifty thousand dollars' worth of sea-to-sea publicity absolutely free!

GRAVEL, *impressed*:   Of course, if you . . .

ROBERGE: From now on, Pierre my boy, if you have any little problems don't waste time crying to little Jesus; call on me.

GRAVEL, *to* O'BRIEN: I suppose this is what happens when you sell your soul to the Devil.

ROBERGE: Don't worry, everyone knows he pays on the dotted line. But better make up your mind to sell you're already hooked, anyway.

GRAVEL: Not that badly.

ROBERGE, *to* O'BRIEN: You know what he reminds me of? An old maid, crazy for love, who won't get married for fear it's a sin.

GRAVEL: Yes: but she still has the right to wonder if at her age she's got enough experience to make a go of it.

ROBERGE: I wouldn't worry about the old girl's technique—she's been necking ever since she knew how!

GRAVEL: Joking apart, the very thought of stepping into Duranceau's shoes is enough to give me cold feet.

ROBERGE: Never mind the modesty: you can go a lot further than he could.

GRAVEL: That's easily said.

ROBERGE: Between you and me and the doorpost, for the Liberal Party this could be an ill wind that blows good.

GRAVEL: How come?

ROBERGE: If you put Pearson on the rack, he'd admit through his tears he wasn't all that sold on Duranceau.

GRAVEL, *incredulous*: You think so?

ROBERGE: I know so. You see, Duranceau had him by the short hair. That guy could get elected upside down or sideways. Prove to the voters he was a grade-A racketeer, they'd vote him in with the biggest majority ever! You want to know what Duranceau is? He's an operator. And the worst of it is he gambles even when he's out of chips. You saw that neat bit of figure-skating in Parliament when Diefenbaker broke the Imperial Steel business a couple of months ago?

GRAVEL: Hear that? He'll be saying the same thing about me in a couple of years—after I've had my hemorrhage.

ROBERGE: Look, Pearson's had his bellyful of the

19

scandal-boys. He's fed to the teeth with second-raters with a past imperfect! Then along comes you—innocent as a new-born babe.

GRAVEL: Innocent—you can say that again. Not one half-hour's experience in Parliament.

ROBERGE: What's the difference! It's not the Minister who does the work, it's his Civil Servants; you know that. The best lawyer in Montreal . . .

GRAVEL, *indicating* O'BRIEN: After him.

ROBERGE: A Q.C., with an Irish wife. . .

GRAVEL: Irish . . . after a fashion: back four generations.

ROBERGE: In this racket, my boy, you put on your best pose; that'll mean a lot in Toronto. And that's not all: you're a model husband.

GRAVEL: Don't ever let my wife know!

ROBERGE: A chip off an old Liberal block. . .

GRAVEL: I may be the last of the line. When you see what our young folks are up to these days. . .

ROBERGE: A dedicated federalist, practising what you preach . . . (*Calling to* O'BRIEN *to witness*) God's truth, isn't it?

GRAVEL, *to* ROBERGE: Listen: I'm a federalist all right. But not under any and all conditions. That clear?

ROBERGE: Absolutely.

GRAVEL, *serious*: I have firm convictions on that subject, and I stick to my convictions.

ROBERGE: Oh? Politics and principles aren't mutually exclusive, you know. Give a little, take a little—we're not barbarians!

GRAVEL: I don't believe in separatism. . . . In my view it would be an unspeakably stupid course. A catastrophe which would plunge the province into everlasting misery.

ROBERGE: Look, you're preaching to the converted!

GRAVEL: But that doesn't mean French-Canada should let itself be steamrollered by the Establishment like so much asphalt.

ROBERGE: If that ever happened, you can count on me, I'd be on your side. I've got principles too, you know—you're not the only one. I've been doing the watchdog act for seventeen years now.

GRAVEL: This speech of mine tomorrow, it's got some eye-openers in it. I'd better warn you there'll be a few uncomfortable moments for some people in Toronto, London and all points west.

The Telephone rings.

O'BRIEN, *answering*: Hello? . . . Just a moment, please. (*To* ROBERGE) It's for you.

ROBERGE, *on the phone*: Roberge here. . . . What? . . . Are you sure? . . . Okay. [*He hangs up. After a pause.*] Duranceau . . .

GRAVEL: All over?

ROBERGE: Five minutes ago.

GRAVEL, *his hand to his forehead momentarily*: Poor fellow.

ROBERGE: Don't worry about him: he's already in heaven.

GRAVEL: Poor fellow.

ROBERGE, *coming to* GRAVEL: Now it all depends on you.

GRAVEL, *still shaken by the news*: Then go away and let me think.

ROBERGE: Sure, think all you like . . . but tell me now, you'll take it on, eh?

GRAVEL, *gently pushing him toward the door*: I've

told you: I want to talk it over with my wife. [*Indicating* O'BRIEN] With him, too.

ROBERGE: Then make it quick, please? It's all pretty straightforward.

GRAVEL: For you, maybe.

ROBERGE: If you'll do it. If you won't—I say "if," notice—if you're fool enough to refuse, I have to know damn quick. You understand?

GRAVEL: I do.

ROBERGE: I can't keep Fournier on ice forever. Not to mention those reporters—they'll be on my back the minute I step into the Windsor.

GRAVEL: All right. . . . But just give me a breathing space!

ROBERGE: Meantime I'll collect the necessary twenty-five signatures from eager-beaver supporters for your nomination slip tomorrow morning.

GRAVEL: Mine . . . or Fournier's?

ROBERGE: Don't worry. I'll get both slips signed at once; that'll keep them confused as long as possible. I don't want the cat let out of the bag before the eleven p.m. news. Sunday night, everybody's home— you hit the jackpot.

GRAVEL, *wearily*:   All right. . . . Do what you think best.

ROBERGE: Anyway, I'll call you around eight-thirty. Just to ask how your wife is: right?

GRAVEL: Later than that; she won't be here till eight-twenty.

ROBERGE: Listen! I'll bet you three cigars she'll go along—as quick as you can say "Mister Minister"!

GRAVEL, *pushing him out the door*:   My God, will you get out of here?

ROBERGE *disappears but immediately returns.*

ROBERGE: And don't forget to have your secretary
shoot me that *curriculum vitae*, huh?

He disappears, this time for good.

SCENE THREE

*The silence contrasts sharply with the verbose departure
of* ROBERGE.

GRAVEL, *putting his hand to his head*:   Now I will have
a drink! I need it!

O'BRIEN: I can see why.

GRAVEL, *helping himself to a drink*:   You?

O'BRIEN: No thanks.

GRAVEL: He didn't exactly give you the floor!

O'BRIEN: It's not such a bad idea for one of the pair of
us to observe while the other holds forth. It's a
technique we've used to advantage in court.

GRAVEL: Where the more useful partner is often the
silent one. All of which means I'm relying on you to
guide me through this fog. Because . . . well, it must
be plain my compass has gone haywire.

A pause. GRAVEL *sits in an armchair and ponders,
his head in his hands.*

O'BRIEN: As far as the office is concerned, let me
reassure you right away. You're really the lead tenor
in our troupe. So I'd be stretching it if I said we
wouldn't miss you. But we'll manage. What's more,
it's never done a legal firm any harm to lend one of
its big guns to the Government.

GRAVEL: Obviously.

O'BRIEN: All right then: I've a question—a most important one—and I know you'll answer, as always, without beating about the bush. Are you really interested in going into this?

GRAVEL: To tell the whole truth, I'm dying to. I was noncommittal in front of Roberge to see if they were really interested in having me. But I'm dying to!

O'BRIEN: No mistake, you're a real French Canadian!

GRAVEL: Politics have fascinated me ever since I was five years old. From the day I saw my father place a little plaster bust of Sir Wilfrid Laurier on the sideboard right beside the statue of the Sacred Heart. My poor father! What would he say if he were around today?—a man who died believing himself a statesman, all because he'd been an alderman for twelve years!

O'BRIEN: So the adventure intrigues you.

GRAVEL: You know, for twenty years I've been mixed up in the backstage power-plays. Twenty years of making decisions for others!

O'BRIEN: Now you want to take your place in the front line!

GRAVEL: There comes a boiling-point. You feel like a fake eunuch hiding in a harem: he watches his master fail more often than not, and he thinks "Hell, I could do better than that!" That's hardly the analogy your sister'd draw, but . . .

O'BRIEN, *unable to control his laughter*: I get the picture!

GRAVEL, *smiling*: I'm sure you do.

O'BRIEN: About Louise . . . The possibility must often have occurred to her.

GRAVEL: In my courting days, I used to talk as much politics as love to her. Besides, we've pretty well always seen things eye-to-eye. It comes from an old habit started during our honeymoon, of enjoying th same pleasures at the same moment. That's how it still is, most of the time—except maybe the odd night she drags me to the Symphony!

O'BRIEN: Louise is an intelligent woman. She's well-read; she'd be an asset to you anywhere.

GRAVEL: I've no qualms; when Parliament opens, she won't need to wear mink to get noticed. That's what I often tell the boys: "Pick a woman like your mother—an attractive girl with a strong enough personality to keep up with you on the road to success. . . ."

O'BRIEN: And the boys?

GRAVEL: Let's start with Larry. No problem there.

O'BRIEN: He's a well-balanced kid.

GRAVEL: Besides, his one consuming passion for the past couple of months has been writing songs: can you imagine it?—words and music!

O'BRIEN: So that's why he was hinting about a guitar for his birthday.

GRAVEL: Spoil him like that and you'll be his pal for life! My contribution—if I don't want to be left behind—could be the chair to put his foot on!

O'BRIEN: Fame and fortune, here we come!

GRAVEL, *after a laugh*: Seriously, it's good I sent him to Loyola to get his degree in English. My reason at first was purely sentimental: those few drops of Irish blood from his mother. But when I think of the nationalist brain-washing his brother got at Brébeuf, I'm damn glad I did.

O'BRIEN: Yes, André is . . . well . . . a tougher proposition.

GRAVEL: He's a dark horse, that boy. You'll never saddle him without a tussle. Remember his reaction when I offered him a job with the firm last June— after he'd passed his Bar exam? "Thank you, that's

25

very kind of you: when I'm ready I'll let you know."

O'BRIEN: He's a Gravel all right!

GRAVEL: You said it.

O'BRIEN: I get the impression this won't exactly go down like a glass of milk.

GRAVEL: If it does he'll have a few burps after. Oh, I tell you, the spat we had last week! He found out I was giving the talk in Toronto and he hit the roof. . . . Wanted me to cancel out. . . . Said I could use the campaign as an excuse.

O'BRIEN: Why?

GRAVEL: Apparently it embarrasses him with his separatist friends, his father going to talk about Federalism—in the other language—on the other side of the Quebec border. Well finally I got mad. I told him bluntly, "Mind your own business! D'you think I'd enjoy it if my friends knew you were demonstrating against the Queen on her Quebec visit? I don't object when you stick to your convictions, according to your lights: allow me the same courtesy. You can bury me when I'm dead—not before." That disarmed him; he came up to me and said, "I want you to know if I'm ever a complication in your life it won't be intentional; and I'll be unhappier about it than you." He's no cry-baby, but he almost had tears in his eyes. To make up we played a game of chess. I was watching every move, thinking, "He'll let himself be beaten so he can be forgiven." I was wrong: in no time I was checkmate.

O'BRIEN: That's the reassuring thing about André: his political ideas are still a little mixed-up, but he admires and respects his father.

GRAVEL: Any serious objections his mother has I'd have to take into account. My career is Louise's career. But I'm not going to wait for the approval of a twenty-three-year-old son who already does as he pleases with or without my blessing.

O'BRIEN: He's bright enough to see the force of logic, especially after that little lesson you gave him.

GRAVEL: If he doesn't buy it, that's just too bad. And yet, I admit it would bother me . . . because . . .

O'BRIEN: Because you try to show it as little as possible . . . but you've got a soft spot for that boy.

GRAVEL: I'm afraid you're right. What the heck!—he impresses me, the little bugger! Any more, and I'd stand in awe of him.

O'BRIEN: If you want my opinion, it's mutual.

GRAVEL: Yes . . . apart from the minor detail of politics, we get along pretty well. Specially when we go off alone, just him and me, on the lake in the sailboat. There, Paul, we're not two beings, we're one. We tack and luff like a dream: it would take a typhoon to upset us. I remember the first time we sailed off together. He was four years old; standing between my legs as we were speeding along like an arrow. He turns round and says, "Daddy, you're the mains'l: I'm the little jib!" "Yes," I said, "but you'll grow up, while I shrink more and more; and one day we'll have changed places." And hugging my knee he said, "No! For me, you'll always be the mains'l!" The little son-of-a-gun! I could've thrown him in, just for the sheer joy of pulling him out again!

O'BRIEN, *after a pause*:   What's he up to these days?

GRAVEL: We haven't seen much of him this summer; he's been tooting around on his scooter from one end of the province to the other. I think he's finding himself.

O'BRIEN: He will find himself someday. He was admitted to the Bar before he was twenty-three—that's exceptional.

27

GRAVEL: With a 91% average, it is: they tell me no one's hit that in twelve years.

O'BRIEN: Then he can still afford to idle away a few months without wrecking his career.

GRAVEL: Sure. You watch: he'll join the firm when he's run through the two thousand dollars your father left him.

O'BRIEN: That's what he's living on?

GRAVEL: He's much too proud to make me pay for his wild oats—now more than ever, as a matter of fact: I gather he's been in love for the last six months. A bright little thing—tempting as a French pastry— and she seems to have fallen for him head over heels. He lets himself be run after, but his mother claims he's far gone.

O'BRIEN: Marriage'll bring him back to earth.

GRAVEL: There's nothing like it to settle a youngster down.

The SECRETARY *enters from the study with the text of the speech in her hand.*

SECRETARY: Excuse me, Mr. Gravel.

GRAVEL: Yes?

SECRETARY: I've read through it. . . .

GRAVEL: Is it bad enough for you?

SECRETARY: If you ask me, you're really going to jolt them.

GRAVEL: That's exactly what I want to do.

SECRETARY: But there are a couple of passages you might clear up for me.

GRAVEL: Shoot.

SECRETARY, *indicating a place in the text*: Here, for instance: I can't make out this word.

GRAVEL, *peering at the text*: "Chasm."

SECRETARY: Of course!

GRAVEL, *to* O'BRIEN: Listen to this. [*Reading*] "Get this straight, gentlemen: unless we—and that includes you too—unless we bridge the chasm of Quebec's unhappiness with the present state of Confederation, Canada will fall apart, you can be dead sure! And you, gentlemen, not the Separatists from Quebec, will be mainly responsible for that calamity."

O'BRIEN: That's calling a spade a spade.

GRAVEL: No sir, weasel words are not my style!

SECRETARY, *indicating another passage*: And there's a blank here: something missing in the sentence, I think.

GRAVEL, *reading*: "If I am right in affirming with . . ." [*Getting it*] Oh yes!—I couldn't remember the name of the mental giant who said that. Just put ". . . with the philosopher." That's one of those words that always sound good.

SECRETARY: Fine.

GRAVEL, *to* O'BRIEN: Here's another titbit. [*Reading*] "If I am right in affirming, with the philosopher, that those who are perpetually unsatisfied are the motors of society, where do you think your present attitude of perpetual satisfaction with yourself will lead this country in the end?" [*To* O'BRIEN, *giving the sheet back to the* SECRETARY.] The rest you can read someday in our Canadian history books.

O'BRIEN: You're really letting them have it, aren't you!

GRAVEL: If their backs are properly up, I'll ask for police protection to get back to the airport.

SECRETARY: That's all. Do you mind if I work at the office? I can mimeograph it there.

GRAVEL: Good idea.

SECRETARY: I'll bring everything back around nine: will that be soon enough?

GRAVEL: Plenty.

The SECRETARY *takes a moment to arrange the papers.*

O'BRIEN: It sounds for all the world like a Separatist speech!

GRAVEL: Just about. The first person I want to get it across to is André. He must understand that "valiant defenders of our threatened country" can be found outside the fort as well as inside.

O'BRIEN: It might help him accept your candidacy.

The doorbell sounds.

GRAVEL, *to the* SECRETARY, *who is about to put her coat on in the hallw*ay: Oh: Miss Martin, would you get the door? If it's an interloper, use your well-known tact.

SECRETARY: Right. [*She disappears toward the door.*]

GRAVEL: Fundamentally it's a question of words. The Separatists get stirred up telling themselves the bottle's half empty. . . . We try to unstir them by telling them it's half full.

O'BRIEN: Both of you are really after the same thing: only there's a difference of opinion about the means.

SCENE FOUR

NICOLE *enters, unseen by* GRAVEL *and* O'BRIEN.

GRAVEL, *to* O'BRIEN, *following his train of thought*: The way I see it, what's keeping me and André apart is as stupid as a religious war between Christians in the middle of an Ecumenical Council.

O'BRIEN: Just about.

NICOLE: Hello, Mr. Gravel.

GRAVEL: And hello to you, Nicole! You know, this is the first time I've ever been frightened by a pretty girl! [*To* O'BRIEN] Paul, you've met André's girl friend?

O'BRIEN: Indeed I have.

NICOLE: Mr. O'Brien . . . [*To* GRAVEL] You'll probably think I'm absolutely shameless, but I was walking by your house . . .

GRAVEL, *smiling*: Accidentally?

NICOLE: No. I'll be perfectly frank: I did it as deliberately as I could. It's embarrassing to admit, but I'm just a poor little girl running after your son—imagine!

GRAVEL: Some guys have all the luck.

The SECRETARY *re-enters, to reclaim her brief-case.*

NICOLE: We were supposed to spend the day together, but he called me around two to say he had to go to Granby—something urgent, he said—but he'd call me as soon as he got back.

GRAVEL: Well!

NICOLE: I saw his scooter by the garage, so I figured he must be here.

GRAVEL: Sorry, but if he is, I haven't seen him.

NICOLE: Are you serious?

GRAVEL: Yes ma'am! But he can't be far away. Take off your coat and we'll look for him.

NICOLE, *doing so*: Okay.

SECRETARY, *ready to go*: Excuse me . . . but I was crossing the park on my way here and I saw André there . . . on a bench. He was sort of meditating: you know, his head in his hands.

NICOLE: That's odd. . . .

GRAVEL: It's his meditation time: he does it every Sunday. Meanwhile, you go up to his room and hunt for that textbook you mentioned on the phone. I haven't had a minute.

NICOLE: Good! Because . . . to tell the truth I don't really need it. It was just an excuse to find out about André; the exam was last week.

GRAVEL, *to* O'BRIEN, *breaking into a laugh*: If all our witnesses in court were as frank, how simple a lawyer's job would be!

NICOLE: A girl in love will try anything.

GRAVEL: True enough.

NICOLE: But surely I'm disturbing you. I feel like a kitten who's skidded into a bowling alley.

GRAVEL: Your timing is perfect. You can keep your future uncle company while I go up and shave. In all this whirl I got no chance this morning. [*He goes upstairs.*]

NICOLE: Don't dress up for me, huh? [*To* O'BRIEN] I hope I'm not depressing you: I'm a little . . . lugubrious tonight.

O'BRIEN, *smiling*: It doesn't show at all.

NICOLE: That's just it: with this face of mine, it never does. I could be dying of a broken heart right under your nose and you'd swear I was on my way to a picnic! It's hell!

O'BRIEN: You've got a real problem there.

NICOLE: I wonder what's got into him?—sitting on a park bench, and with his head in his hands! Something's bugging him.

O'BRIEN: He may be figuring out how to propose to you.

NICOLE: If that's it, there's no need to beat his brains out: I'd say Yes like that, with both my arms round his neck. But he won't get round to that subject—not for ages.

O'BRIEN: In his own good time, he will.

NICOLE: Meanwhile it's a drag. I was so happy to be spending this Sunday with him. . . specially 'cause he told me last week I'd better get used to the idea of not seeing him for a few months.

O'BRIEN: Oh?

NICOLE: Said he was going on a long trip. . . .

O'BRIEN: Really?

NICOLE: . . .and when he came back maybe we'd talk about serious things—if I went along with his reasons for going there.

O'BRIEN: He didn't give you any details?

NICOLE: No. He was as close as a clam. All he let out was that this was terribly important for his self-determination.

O'BRIEN: Could be a term of study abroad. . . .

NICOLE: Personally, I think he plans to go and work for UNICEF, in Africa or somewhere. He's always talking about principles—sacrificing personal comfort for the good of underdeveloped nations.

O'BRIEN: An admirable sentiment.

NICOLE: You know what I'd do? I'd follow him to the ends of the earth, come hell or high water.

O'BRIEN: A single man can get along more easily than a couple when the going is rough.

NICOLE: Maybe. And I gather milk is hard to get for babies in those countries. You see, there's no rush about getting married, just so long as I know I'll be married to him.

O'BRIEN: As far as you're concerned the matter is settled?

33

NICOLE: Oh yes! From the first moment I saw him, a year ago this month. It was at a student election meeting at college. When I walked in he was in the middle of his campaign speech. He was irresistible! A genuine leader, Mr. O'Brien. After the speech, I went up to him and solemnly declared: "You're the man we need!" I used the plural, I said "we," but if I'd been less of a hypocrite I'd 've used the singular. He looked deep into my eyes, touched my cheek, and said in a voice that thrilled me to the core: "Then canvass for me; it's your duty."

O'BRIEN: And I bet you were a great canvasser.

NICOLE: You should have seen me! Only I was out of breath for about six months trying to keep bumping into him accidentally, in every corridor in the place, before he finally got around to cornering me in the elevator to 4B.

O'BRIEN: He was playing hard to get, the way his father did with my sister.

NICOLE: Someday he'll end up loving me back. After all, I have most of the required qualifications. In the first place I'm pretty. Maybe you don't think so, but my authority is André himself.

O'BRIEN: Then it must be true.

NICOLE: That's it, as far as I'm concerned. Even if the whole world thought me a fright, I'd never be able to work up a complex about that. In the second place, my I.Q. is only three points lower than his.

O'BRIEN: Ideal!

NICOLE: When we showed each other our tests, I was terribly afraid I'd show up brighter than him!

O'BRIEN: And in the third place?

NICOLE: In high heels, I come up to his ear. That makes me a dreamy proportion for a boy his size. Finally—I forget what number we're up to—but the main point is, I love him like a f . . . No, not like a fool: that would mean nothing. It's more like an extremely clear-thinking woman who knows a real man when she meets one—and you don't meet them every day, believe you me.

O'BRIEN: And yet André's far from perfect.

NICOLE: Oh, you're so right!

O'BRIEN: He's inclined to be rather . . . stubborn at times.

NICOLE: I'll go further than that. I'd say at times he's pushy. But that's just what I want in my type of man: let him push, but let him by! To me, that's what makes him attractive: you know? It's like a woman: if you ask me, she should be a bit unpredictable if she wants to hold her man.

O'BRIEN: That's wisdom indeed.

NICOLE: Maybe I'm not unpredictable enough—'cause it's not easy, let me tell you, to get him off the centre of the road. Though there are nights when he designs zigzags that're kind of reassuring for a little girl who has her doubts.

GRAVEL, *who has been listening for a moment from mid-stairway, knotting his tie*: Don't you worry, young lady, the day will come when he'll fall into your tender trap. [*He is down by now.*]

NICOLE: You think so?

GRAVEL: His mother—who can get more out of him than I can—was telling me what André said about you, a few days ago.

NICOLE: That I'm an engaging little bit of fluff?

GRAVEL: No. He told her—and I quote as faithfully as memory serves—"With Nicole, I'm waiting to propose until circumstances let her know me for what I am. Then if she still wants me, there'll never be another woman in my life."

35

NICOLE, *elated*:   I could kiss you for that! [*She spontaneously hugs* GRAVEL.]

GRAVEL: This is definitely my lucky day! Today I get to embrace not only a pretty girl but a new career—you realize that?

NICOLE, *still moved by the revelation she's just had*: Oh, I'm so grateful!

GRAVEL: Hey! Listen to me! I'm giving you the scoop of the week. Try and enjoy it a little.

NICOLE: All right, but make it quick so I can get back to enjoying what else you told me.

GRAVEL, *proud of his little newsbreak*:   Well then, I'll come right to the point: I'm being offered a cabinet post in Ottawa.

NICOLE, *shrugging*:   Oh?

GRAVEL: It doesn't impress you any more than that?

NICOLE: You want a truthful answer or a polite one?

GRAVEL, *amused*:   I get a hint you favour the truth.

NICOLE: Yes. Politeness is one virtue I wasn't born with: I caught it from the nuns at the convent.

GRAVEL, *to* O'BRIEN: Shall we opt for truth, Paul?

O'BRIEN: Always.

NICOLE: Well, I'll admit I'd 've been more impressed with such news . . . let's say in 1867.

GRAVEL: In other words, you think it's not exactly in the swim to be a Federal Minister?

NICOLE: Right. A Provincial Minister . . . maybe. There you could possibly contribute to the . . . flowering of Quebec.

GRAVEL: It wouldn't be altogether out of the question?

NICOLE: Exactly. As things stand, I think it's a shame to see an intelligent man like you . . .

GRAVEL: Thank you.

NICOLE: . . . but a man with no time to lose, considering . . . [*She hesitates.*]

GRAVEL: . . . considering that he's on the verge of old age?

NICOLE, *ever honest*:   Exactly. . . . To go and sit around in Ottawa, playing Tic-Tac-Toe with the Conservatives.

GRAVEL: That's all I'll do there, you think?

NICOLE: Politics red, politics blue . . . mostly rainbow-coloured politics. . . .

GRAVEL: Look: I grant you Confederation is sick, but we must try to save it.

NICOLE: Before you go, read up on artificial respiration: you'll need it.

GRAVEL, *teasing her*:   But would you perhaps admit you don't know all there is to know about federal politics?

NICOLE: I don't know the first thing about it. But maybe that'll make up for all the people who go round saying flatly that Independence for Quebec is an impossibility before they've really studied the question. [*As* GRAVEL *bursts into laughter*] Now: if you'd like to talk about something else go right ahead; that's all I have to say on that subject.

GRAVEL: Well, young lady, if André's children are as frank and cute as you are, I know one grandfather who'll get a great bang out of nattering with them!

NICOLE: Talking about André, what on earth could he mean by saying, "I'll propose when she knows me for what I am?" I know him inside out already.

The telephone rings.

SCENE FIVE

O'BRIEN, *answering the phone*:   Hello? . . . One moment, please. [*To* GRAVEL] Long distance from

37

Ottawa. [*On phone*] May I ask who's calling? . . .
[*Impressed, to* GRAVEL] The Prime Minister's residence!

GRAVEL, *taking the phone*: Yes . . . Speaking . . . I'll
wait. [*Covering the mouthpiece*] Good old Roberge!
He kept his word!

O'BRIEN: There's his famous proof.

GRAVEL, *on phone*: Yes. . . . How do you do, Mr.
Pearson? . . . It's mighty good of you to take the
trouble to call. . . . It's a damn shame! He was an excellent man indeed. . . . Well, as you can easily guess,
I am swept off my feet. Personally, I consider the
proposal an honour and a duty I can hardly refuse.
But, as a matter of principle, I want to get a seal of
approval from my wife. One of our sons is driving
her from our country place. So we'll have a little
caucus together and take a vote: I am liberal minded
not only in politics but also within the family, you
know . . . [ANDRÉ *appears in the hallway*.] Oh, I'm
quite confident she'll be thrilled. . . .

NICOLE, *sotto voce seeing* ANDRÉ: André! [*She runs
to him.*]

GRAVEL, *still on phone*: I do understand.

NICOLE, *low, hanging on* ANDRÉ'S *arm*: I saw your
scooter at the door, so I came in: you're not angry
with me?

GRAVEL, *on phone*: There's no time to lose, for sure.

ANDRÉ, *kissing* NICOLE'S *tresses*: I wanted to see you
alone, but since you're here . . .

GRAVEL, *visibly flattered, still on the phone*: It's mighty
good of you to tell me so: the path is now much
clearer for me. . . .

NICOLE, *low, to* ANDRÉ: It's the Prime Minister calling
your father from Ottawa. [*Without enthusiasm*] If
you knew what for.

38

GRAVEL, *on phone*:   Oh! I'm quite certain that Roberge
   will get an official word of acceptance within an hour
   or so. And again, thank you for calling, Mr. Pearson.
   . . . Goodbye! [*To* O'BRIEN, *as he hangs up*] You
   know what he said to me? "Pierre, we have big plans
   for you!"

O'BRIEN: That reassures you, doesn't it?

GRAVEL: You bet it does. [*Turning, he notices* ANDRÉ.]
   Well I'll be. . . . Evening, André. You'll never guess
   what's happened!

ANDRÉ: I know.

GRAVEL: I hope you're going to congratulate me?

ANDRÉ *shrugs "No."*

GRAVEL, *astonished*:   What's this!

ANDRÉ, *after a strained silence*:   You can't accept.

GRAVEL, *a murmur, thinking he has misunderstood*:
   Uh?

ANDRÉ: You have to refuse: you've no choice.

GRAVEL, *his wrath rising*:   Now listen to me: you're not
   going to revive the little scene we had about the
   speech, are you? Because—

ANDRÉ: This time it's a lot more serious. [*Pointing to
   the newspaper which* O'BRIEN *was reading at curtain-
   rise*] You're aware of what happened in Quebec last
   night?

GRAVEL, *suddenly concerned*:   About the bomb? I know
   what the papers reported.

ANDRÉ, *each word painful for him*:   I came to tell you
   it's no isolated incident. It's the first coup in an organized campaign.

GRAVEL: What?

ANDRÉ: The first of many, each night in a different city,
   until election day.

GRAVEL, *afraid to grasp it*:   How do you know?

ANDRÉ: More than three weeks ago, it was decided

Montreal would get it next Saturday. But, on account
of what you've just been offered, that'd be too late:
the plan has to be changed. You understand?

GRAVEL, *low*: What have you got to do with all this?

ANDRÉ: The one who was to do the job six days from
now will have to do it tonight. So you'd be fore-
warned right away, and not make the disastrous mistake of accepting . . .

GRAVEL, *stammering*: You're the one who . . .

ANDRÉ: Because anyway your party would drop a
candidate whose son was in prison on voting day,
after he'd turned himself in for so-called criminal
activities.

GRAVEL *looks at* O'BRIEN *as if to reassure himself
that he is not having a nightmare*: NICOLE *throws her-
self in an armchair, her head in her hands.*

GRAVEL, *in a daze, during the silence which follows*:
No . . .

O'BRIEN, *totally stupefied himself*: This is absurd!

ANDRÉ, *unable to hide his own uneasiness*: For weeks
I'd foreseen everything . . . except what happened to
you today.

GRAVEL, *crushed, murmurs*: André . . . André . . . You
can't do this to me!

ANDRÉ, *sincere*: Forgive me. If only I'd known . . . I
wonder what I would have done. . . . Now it's too
late.

NICOLE: Couldn't you have told me?

ANDRÉ, *shaking his head*: Regulations. [*To* GRAVEL,
regaining his courage] Now you know . . . I must go.

O'BRIEN, *trying to persuade him to stay*: André . . .
think: you're not going to ruin your father's career
for a senseless thing like that?

ANDRÉ, *hardening*: The only senseless thing is this situation, happening as suddenly as it has. The rest is still worthwhile.

O'BRIEN: But you've just admitted you're not sure what you'd have done if you'd known beforehand.

ANDRÉ: I don't know what I would've done to save him the injury I'm doing him. But nothing essential would have been changed.

O'BRIEN, *panic forcing him to raise his voice involuntarily*: At least explain yourself—you must!

ANDRÉ: I didn't come here to debate: I came to warn you—that's all.

GRAVEL, *coming out of his daze, going to* ANDRÉ: You think I'm just going to let you go?

ANDRÉ, *miserable but resolute*: It's out of my hands, don't you see?

GRAVEL, *nearly losing his self-control*: I ought to hit you for the first time in my life!

ANDRÉ, *intractable*: That wouldn't get you very far.

GRAVEL, *crushed*: You imbecile!

ANDRÉ, *standing up to him*: That won't settle anything either!

They stand face-to-face, like two enemies. O'BRIEN *touches* GRAVEL'S *arm and silently conveys the message:* "Let me handle this." *Still dazed by the shock,* GRAVEL *retreats.*

O'BRIEN, *reaching out*: André, listen to me for a moment. If you find I've nothing worthwhile to say, you can leave in thirty seconds.

ANDRÉ, *still breathless*: Go ahead.

O'BRIEN, *choosing his words carefully*: Bomb throwers are of two kinds: the weak, who destroy to attract attention, because they feel they've no other way of

41

letting the world know they exist. Forced to justify themselves, they run away, afraid they'll be pricked like balloons.

ANDRÉ: And the others.

O'BRIEN: They do battle, sure of their cause. Now: where do you stand?

ANDRÉ: You're too shrewd to think I'd 've waited till now to know where I stand.

O'BRIEN: A pat on the back from buddies already sold on your ideas is no proof whatever of their validity; obviously they won't cavil.

ANDRÉ: I could be right beyond cavil, and still you'd refuse to admit it.

O'BRIEN: Forget about us. This is your last chance to prove to yourself that your cause is worth the exorbitant price you're eager to pay for it.

ANDRÉ: That won't change a thing, as I've said.

O'BRIEN: On the contrary. If your conscience is clear still, you'll go out of here a stronger man. And I for one will be forced, in spite of everything, to keep my respect for you. Otherwise . . .

ANDRÉ: I'm going anyway.

O'BRIEN: Otherwise, it's your tragedy. Your father's fate is being decided tonight—but first and foremost it's your fate which hangs in the balance now. Yours . . . [*Indicating* NICOLE] and perhaps hers, too. If we are beyond salvage, she certainly isn't. Like us, she knows both too much and too little to judge you. Unless you don't care about her grief, and the way she feels about you.

NICOLE: André . . . for my sake.

There is a pause while he considers his decision.

NICOLE: Please, André. . . . Please!

ANDRÉ: All right. [*Regaining his aplomb*] I accept the challenge. [*To* NICOLE] For you.

NICOLE: Thank you.

ANDRÉ, *to* GRAVEL *and* O'BRIEN: But the battle will be bloody, I warn you.

GRAVEL: I'm sure it will.

O'BRIEN: The stakes are too high to pull the punches.

A clock offstage chimes eight o'clock.

ANDRÉ: One word of advice: don't yield to the temptation to keep me here any longer than it takes, in hopes you can prevent the scandal. [*As much for his father as for* O'BRIEN] It's eight o'clock. If I'm not where I ought to be by nine-twenty, it's been set up for someone else to take my place. But I'm still the one who'll turn himself in. The leader of the movement could never back out like a coward.

O'BRIEN, *after a shocked pause*:   The leader?

ANDRÉ: You heard me. Now, fire ahead. [*Starting to to take off his coat*] What would you like to know?

The curtain falls.

ACT TWO

SCENE SIX

At curtain-rise, the characters are in the same positions they occupied at the end of Act One: there has been no lapse in the action.

ANDRÉ, *as he finishes taking off his coat*: All right: shoot! [*To his father*] Your last word was "imbecile." Go on: that's the classic opening for a dialogue with a Separatist.

GRAVEL, *vehemently*: Yes, an imbecile! Or at least a crackpot. If you're as intelligent as you think, you ought to realize that this blessed violence of yours—which you call patriotism—has already been tried and found wanting pathetically!

ANDRÉ: Yes, a good tool can be misused.

O'BRIEN: Those very people you're trying to win over to your cause, André . . . don't you understand that the surest way of losing them is to explode bombs that might kill their children in the streets?

GRAVEL: And for the sake of a fiasco like that, you're ready to rot in jail, as other lunatics are doing right now?

ANDRÉ: You condemn them; but history will judge them on appeal with the objectivity you lack.

GRAVEL: I have no doubt about the verdict.

ANDRÉ: Nor I.

GRAVEL: It'll still be clear they were sadly mistaken.

44

ANDRÉ: In the means used, yes. Like the patriots of 1837. But face it: the cause of this new rebellion is every bit as legitimate as theirs, because it's one and the same.

O'BRIEN: With this essential difference: those rebels were killing British soldiers, not their defenceless countrymen.

ANDRÉ: We'll see we make as much noise as they did, but without sacrificing lives.

O'BRIEN: Oh sure! Hell is paved with intentions like that.

GRAVEL: Go into the prisons and ask the deflated little heroes who planted bombs in letter boxes and armouries if it was their intention to kill one man and maim another for life!

ANDRÉ: As I said, apart from what's happened to you today, my plan took everything into account.

O'BRIEN: Your plan?

ANDRÉ: Yes. I'll take full responsibility.

NICOLE: André . . . won't you tell me what it is? I'm afraid for you.

ANDRÉ: If it's any consolation to you, all right. [*Pulling a piece of paper from his pocket*] In tomorrow morning's mail, the news media will get a copy of this manifesto. [*He hands it to* NICOLE.] If they publish it without distortion, the public will realize there's no danger to them from our fireworks, and they can even enjoy the fun if they feel like it. [*To* NICOLE] Will you read it aloud, please?

NICOLE, *reading*: "We are seventeen companions. We represent a cross-section of society: labouring, professional, farming, student; and each of us lives in a different city of the State of Quebec."

ANDRÉ: When they're all identified, they'll be recognized as men with reputations—spotless until then—

45

for integrity, ability and stability. [*He signals* NICOLE *to continue.*]

NICOLE, *reading*: "Every night until voting day, one of us, each in his own area, will destroy a symbol of British Imperialism, unconnected with private, commercial or industrial property."

ANDRÉ, *commenting*: In fact, a work of art as meaningless as Wolfe's monument.

NICOLE, *reading*: "In every case the target will be a non-habitable structure, so isolated that its destruction will present no risk to neighbouring buildings or their occupants. Moreover, an expert from among the members of the movement will have determined, with the greatest possible precision, the quantity of dynamite in each bomb, so that . . ."

ANDRÉ, *taking over*: ". . . so that the explosion itself affects nothing but the symbol."

NICOLE, *reading*: "In addition—"

ANDRÉ: Listen to this.

NICOLE, *reading*: "In addition, the bomb will be of a type never before used, made to explode within forty-five seconds of being positioned—"

ANDRÉ, *running on by memory, insisting*: ". . . a safety catch making it until then as inoffensive as a grenade. . . ."

NICOLE: "This short-lived bomb will reduce the danger to potential passers-by between priming and detonation, a matter of seconds later."

ANDRÉ: You get the point?

NICOLE, *continuing*: "During this brief interval, the companion will retire no further than essential to ensure his own safety, so he may be in a position to divert, by signs or words, any unforeseen traffic headed in the direction of the target."

ANDRÉ: In short every detail of the affair will show

46

clearly that we did everything possible to protect human life. [*To* NICOLE] And the last paragraph?

NICOLE, *reading*: "Once his mission is accomplished, and if he has not already been arrested on the spot, the companion will add to the protest value of his action that of passive resistance by turning himself in of his own accord. In this way the people of Quebec will realize at once that the sabotage is not the work of a dangerous young punk, as malicious legend would have them believe—"

ANDRÉ: *picking up from memory, and concluding*: ". . . but a young compatriot, in every other way respectful of the established order, and not afraid to face the immediate consequences of his act, a strictly political one arising from deep conviction. [*Between his teeth*] Long live Free Quebec!"

NICOLE, *laying the manifesto down*: Can you rely on your companions, André?

ANDRÉ: As on myself: I spent the summer choosing them, probably more carefully than they pick a Mountie in Ottawa.

O'BRIEN: Still, if one of them talked—

GRAVEL: Only one!

O'BRIEN: . . . despite your confidence in all of them, your whole infallible scheme would collapse.

ANDRÉ: No one will talk.

GRAVEL: Oh, the spirit is willing, but . . .

ANDRÉ: Police sticks are very convincing, I know that. If they managed to frighten one of my men, there's only one name he could reveal: mine. The others he doesn't know. I'm the sole person who knows the whole network.

GRAVEL: And of course, there's no question of you giving in!

ANDRÉ: I'm no braver than the average group-member.

That's why I insisted every one of them choose his own replacement, whose name I do not know, and who'd take his place if something unavoidable came up to prevent him accomplishing his mission at the appointed time and place. So even if I were enough of a coward to name every one of them, the plan would still be executed.

O'BRIEN: By tomorrow—and you know it!—the police will be watching like hawks every possible target.

ANDRÉ: All the way from Hull to the Gaspé? Terrific! Then the world would know that in our lovely French province the reminders of Anglo-Saxon colonialism outnumber the available police.

GRAVEL, *to* ANDRÉ: All right, you've taken precautions.

ANDRÉ: Every conceivable precaution.

GRAVEL: But all the same you're using explosives.

ANDRÉ: Well, of course! You know a better way of knocking over a pile of stone? We can hardly go through the streets with a bulldozer.

GRAVEL: Suppose, despite all your precautions, there was an accident?

ANDRÉ: Then leave your car in the garage. You never know when you'll run over a friend, no matter how good your intentions are.

GRAVEL: That's idiotic!

O'BRIEN: André, you're remembering to forget a fine point which you, as a lawyer, can't honestly ignore.

ANDRÉ: I was waiting to hear your objection, dear colleague.

O'BRIEN: Blaming others won't make it right for you to commit an act the law formally labels a crime.

GRAVEL: Of course!

ANDRÉ: I'm aware of that law: it's the law of the mightiest, so worried about his own skin he won't grant a political suspect the special rights given him in any really civilized country. It's an abominable law, but it's clear. It stipulates that if you're out to deliver your own people, rightly or wrongly, from degrading serf-dom, due process of law—as practised by Her Gra-cious Majesty's government—tosses you in jail, along with common murderers, prostitutes and pyromani-acs. But of course, it's entirely permissible to spread the benefits of American Imperialism by slaughtering thousands of Vietnamese civilians with the blessing of that very same government!

GRAVEL: Duck and weave all you like; the fact remains that the law, good or bad, will condemn you; and you can't escape.

ANDRÉ: Who's talking about escape? Me?—the one who's going to turn himself in tonight? Get this: I know what's in store for me. But the honourable federalist judge who'll hand down my sentence from on high will find me looking him straight in the eye.

O'BRIEN: My poor boy!

ANDRÉ: And he'll be pretty uncomfortable, if the prac-tice of his noble profession hasn't totally atrophied his sense of right and wrong. [*By* NICOLE, *anxious to convince her*] He'll recall that besides the organized justice that makes him condemn me, there's also equity—

GRAVEL: Equity!

ANDRÉ: Equity, pure and simple—which takes into account the circumstances, the true motives, and plain common sense.

GRAVEL: My God!

NICOLE, *who has taken his hand and kissed it*: Sweet-heart, how many eternities will you be away from me? Do you know?

O'BRIEN, *replying for the unhappy* ANDRÉ, *who hesi-tates*: The others'll probably get between six

49

months and a year. But you—if they find out you're
the leader, and they doubtless will—

ANDRÉ: I won't hide it.

O'BRIEN: Then you won't get away with less than two
years in prison.

ANDRÉ: That's what I figured.

NICOLE, *murmering, heartbroken*: Two years! [*She
strokes her cheek with* ANDRÉ'S *hand, choking back
tears.*]

GRAVEL, *going to her*: Yes, two years of liberty lost,
maybe more. The rest of his young manhood ruined
—altogether apart from the anxiety, the harm and
the shame he'll heap on those who love him. And all
that to achieve illegally what he could more easily
achieve by legitimate means.

ANDRÉ, *between his teeth*: If you follow that trail, I
warn you, you'll fall right into a bear trap.

GRAVEL: Oh sure: this musical-comedy plot of yours is
clever enough. But you remind me of those petty
crooks who spend as much time and effort organizing
a five-dollar robbery as they would earning the same
amount of money honestly. What is this masochism
that makes you plunge headlong into violence, when
our democratic system allows anyone to foster the
wildest political theory absolutely legally? Your
weeping and wailing like Jeremiah won't convince
anyone we're living under a dictatorship. If your
Separatist ideas are so terrific, if they're the magic
cure for all that ails us, lay them honestly before the
voters. Who's stopping you? If the people go along
with you, then we'll have to face up to them.

ANDRÉ, *with clenched teeth, waiting till* GRAVEL *finishes
before he counter-attacks*: Oh yes! It would be so
simple! [*Imitating a crier*] O come all ye sympathetic
fools! The political auction is open. Come with your

pennies; dig them out of your piggy banks with a knife; put them down right here beside our fat election kitty and try to match our stakes! Come on, you dear little lambs: fall into our trap and join the game of democracy. We're okay, we've got all the trumps right here in our hand: the police, the army, newspapers, television, radio, liquor, patronage, intimidation, libel, blackmail—and last but not least, the real crusher: beauteous, all-powerful Cash! But play fair, though: no dirty tricks. Violence, physical or verbal, is out: that's our preserve! Because we, the Almighty, will legalize it every time we figure you need a lesson!

GRAVEL, *leaving him for* O'BRIEN: How can you turn off such a Niagara of prejudice?

ANDRÉ, *seizing him again*:   You can't! Because you know damn well that elections in your style democracy aren't won with prayers! Your party, grown fat over a hundred years—where would it be without its lousy treasure chest? Independent parties are poor as church mice—and you know that too. If by some miracle they could ever collect a million bucks to plead their cause, the party in power would come up with ten, twenty, fifty! They only need to tell their backers "Cough up a little or lose the lot!"—and they'd cough up every cent needed. We'd be washed out like so much dirt. And you tell us "No violence"? Then what else do we have to fight with?

O'BRIEN, *raising his voice for the first time, as he feels the ground give way beneath his feet*:   If you think terrorism is the way to educate this province politically, I warn you: you're heading for catastrophe.

ANDRÉ: Excuse me: a nice distinction, if you don't mind! Terrorism, by definition, breeds terror. But the little garage mechanic, all alone on the Plains of

Abraham, who rid the province of an antiquated bird-shit target as humiliating for us as Wolfe's monument, Mark II—and then presented himself at police HQ and politely told the constable on duty: "Would you be so kind as to arrest me? I'm the guy who just pulled the job on the Plains." Do you for one second imagine he terrorized the grand old city of Champlain? Why, at this very minute, every Quebecker who still has an ounce of national pride ought to be laughing up his sleeve. And that's only the beginning. Within a week they'll be laying odds in the taverns, in recreation halls, in beauty parlours—trying to guess which corner of the province will have the fireworks display that night. What with the boring election campaign we're getting right now, when they go to the polls there'll be more talk about Independence than there'll be about Federalism!

O'BRIEN: André, if you're honest, as you claim to be, you'll admit that everything you've said so far shows only that you're ingenious—and that we knew already.

GRAVEL: Just as we know your motives conform to the somewhat dubious moral code you've coined for yourself.

O'BRIEN: But you've said nothing yet that might prove your cause a good one.

ANDRÉ: What's the point?

GRAVEL: But my God, that's the whole question! Any fool can play Don Quixote and go smash his head against windmills.

ANDRÉ, *to* NICOLE: Argue in that vein and they'll drag out every cliché known to man!

GRAVEL: At a time like this, when communications are drawing the five continents closer together than they've ever been throughout history—

52

ANDRÉ, *to* NICOLE: Number one!

GRAVEL: . . . what can you possibly find sensible and inspiring about isolating this province like a medieval ghetto? Why confine your ambitions to Quebec when you have the chance to make your presence felt from one end of this rich country of ours to the other?

ANDRÉ: The grand illusion. Sure! Make our presence felt from Halifax to Victoria, when we can't even take over Montreal! Montreal, the second greatest French city in the world—so they say—where an English population of ten per cent is lord and master of eighty-five per cent of the economy!

The telephone rings and O'BRIEN *answers. Only the end of his reply is audible.*

O'BRIEN: Hello? . . . No, this is O'Brien. . . . We're still waiting for her.

ANDRÉ, *having just had time to draw breath*:   Start de-anglicing Westmount before you send me out to frenchify Assiniboia!

O'BRIEN, *on the phone*:   Where are you? . . . Wait for me, and meanwhile don't do a thing: you might regret it. [*Hangs up. To* GRAVEL] Roberge. I'm going to the Windsor to stall for time.

GRAVEL *shrugs his shoulders as if to say, "What's the good?"*

O'BRIEN, *stopped by* ANDRÉ, *who holds him in the passage and looks him straight in the eye*:   Rest assured, I am no stool pigeon. [*He disengages himself without being rude.*]

ANDRÉ: You see, the coup would still take place, as I've explained.

O'BRIEN: And anyway, you'd turn yourself in. I got the point. [*He goes upstage, where he dons his coat and exits during the dialogue following.*]

GRAVEL, *going to his son*: André, listen to me: I'd be-lieve in Separatism with all my heart too, if I weren't convinced it'd mean economic suicide.

ANDRÉ: That's what you think!

GRAVEL: After enjoying one of the highest standards of living in the world, Quebec would plunge right into the muck for generations to come . . . with all the foul-up brought on by the withdrawal of foreign capital, inflation, the whole rotten mess.

ANDRÉ, *facing up to him*: You're dead certain of that?

GRAVEL: Absolutely certain.

ANDRÉ: A reasonable man like you doesn't arrive at absolute certainty just casually, now, on grave issues like that: you have figures, surveys, statistics to sup-port your views? Or would you, too, by any chance, stoop to demagogy, making statements which suit your purpose but no one has proven to date?

GRAVEL: Look: any economist will tell you that with a population of only six million Quebec could never survive!

ANDRÉ: If the danger is so almighty awful, why not prove it, loud and clear? It's your most resounding objection, the only valid one on the whole. Go right ahead! The problem's been kicking around for half a century. But oh no: you'd never tackle it officially. You'd funk facing the conclusion that a free Quebec could get along every bit as well as Sweden!

GRAVEL: But Sweden's in a completely different context than Quebec: politically it might as well be on an-other planet. . . . [LARRY's *entrance interrupts him*.]

SCENE SEVEN

LARRY, *in the entrance, a suitcase in his hand*: Father . . . Mother's here.

ANDRÉ, *disconcerted by this unexpected arrival, murmuring*: Mother?

GRAVEL: Yes, your poor mother, who could never come within a mile of guessing what's she's walking into.

LARRY *has set down the suitcase, and steps aside as his mother appears, supported by* O'BRIEN. *Then he moves to go out.*

GRAVEL, *coming to his wife*: Louise, you thought you were coming here to share one of the happy moments of my life, but . . .

LOUISE, *interrupting him, overcome*: I know.

O'BRIEN, *explaining to* GRAVEL: I told her.

LOUISE, *sinking into an armchair*: It's insane!

O'BRIEN, *aside to* GRAVEL: Larry's driving me to the Windsor before he puts the car away. [*He goes out, following* GRAVEL'S *vague gesture of acquiescence.*]

GRAVEL, *to* LOUISE: What can we possibly have done to this boy, for him to take revenge by loading us with a cross like this?

LOUISE: André . . . why? . . . Why, my dear?

ANDRÉ, *unhappy and lost*: I didn't think I'd see you here . . . I didn't think . . .

GRAVEL, *sarcastically*: Of course! All you could think of was your own precious conspiracy, which consists of wanting the happiness of your countrymen so badly you start by ruining your own family's!

LOUISE: God knows we never wanted to, but what did we do to hurt you, André?

ANDRÉ: Nothing, Mother. No son was ever loved more.

GRAVEL: And this seems to you the logical way of thanking us?

ANDRÉ, *very close to his mother*: It was . . . what it

55

would do to you . . . I thought of first. That's why I wrote you, a few days ago, things I couldn't put into words now. [*He has taken a letter from his pocket and hands it to her.*] Read it. It might help you understand.

LOUISE, *opening the letter and reading*: "Mother, you remember that summer in the country: I was ten. Every morning I went swimming and you would patiently follow me in the rowboat, encouraging me to beat my distance of the day before. And for your birthday I made you a present of crossing the lake in one go. When I got to the other side, I said proudly: 'Stay with me always, and someday I'll cross the ocean!' You kissed me and said, 'Yes, my boy will cross it one day, the ocean of his life—but first he'll have to learn to grow away from me.' And half crying, I replied that you loved me too much for me to hurt you, ever, by leaving you. And you held me in your arms and made me understand that when the time came for me to go, you would be sad, naturally, but not so sad as you would be if you had to keep in tow an overgrown little boy who lacked the courage to break the apron strings. Mother, they went by too fast, the days of my happy childhood. Now the time has come for me to . . ." [*Her voice breaks.*]

ANDRÉ, *picking it up from memory*: "Now the time has come for me to explore the ocean of my destiny, sorrow and all. If it is strewn with perils beyond your expectation, forgive me any anguish I bring you. I want you to know I shall love you more and more as time goes by, and never stop."

GRAVEL: That's rhetoric! Spun zephyr! You're right: your mother did everything she could to put a head on your shoulders and it's no fault of hers you're acting now like a demented delinquent.

56

LOUISE: My darlings, I was right, then, to worry about the pair of you. Each of you has told me things, in confidence, that made me feel sure a storm was building up between you. Though I never imagined it would strike with such a thunderclap.

GRAVEL: Scandal! That's all he wanted. For months he's been lying in wait for it, like a hunter stalking game. "Pierre Gravel's son, the bomb-thrower, kills two birds with one stone by breaking his federalist father's back at the same time." That's a hell of a neat stunt to brag about! No doubt about you: you're no goddamn cipher!

LOUISE: Pierre, this is no time for insults. More than ever, it's a time for love. Let me have a word with him. [*She caresses* ANDRÉ'S *head as he sits on his knees by her.*] Darling, you were fortunate enough, your brother and you, to grow up in the atmosphere of what you used to call my serenity; but you owe that, mainly, not to me but to your father. From the first day of our life together, he has made me the happiest woman alive. So it was easy for me to love you . . . with all my heart, yes—but as our sons.

ANDRÉ *touches his mother affectionately.*

LOUISE, *continuing*:   To compete with your father in my affection, you had to make your manhood in the image of his. That's how you've become a man. And now you turn against him and want to cover him with shame.

ANDRÉ: Nobody's more unhappy about it than I.

LOUISE: He's an honest man; none more honest.

ANDRÉ: I have no complaints about him, except this thing that's pitting us against each other.

LOUISE: To cause your father such irreparable harm,

your reasons must be extremely serious. If not, you would be guilty of an act. . . I can find no name for.

ANDRÉ: And what about my integrity: do you doubt that?

LOUISE: Of course not: you're just like him. I told you that. That's why I love you so much—you too.

ANDRÉ: Supposing he makes me give in and so does me a greater harm than I could ever do him?

LOUISE: That's not possible.

ANDRÉ: If I couldn't give in without destroying myself, what should I do, according to you—you the one who's always impressed on me that a man should follow his star, whatever the cost?

GRAVEL: Destroying yourself? But that's exactly the monstrous error I want to stop you falling into with your eyes closed!

LOUISE: André, how can you question your father's concern for you? You know he'd do anything in the world to make you happy, Larry and you.

ANDRÉ, *insisting*: Mother, answer me: between a belated career in politics for him, and something that's the whole meaning of life for me, which would you sacrifice?

LOUISE, *hesitating in her honesty*: I don't know. . . .

GRAVEL: It's one thing to toss out grandiose principles like that, but another to back them up.

ANDRÉ: The issue dividing the two of us, Mother, has to do with the future, not the past. It has to do with building what's going to be our world: don't you understand! The world where Nicole and I and the rest of our generation will have to live, long after his generation—which is determined to run everything, to decide everything without us—has gone with the wind. If we differ, too bad! I won't bow down before him. I haven't the right!

GRAVEL: What nonsense!

ANDRÉ, *to his mother*: When the workers rebelled a hundred years ago against being exploited like slaves, the capitalist plutocrats reacted just like him—oh yes! They cried, "Nonsense!" When fifty years ago the women decided to be something more than diaper-changing machines, the males huffed in indignation—oh yes! It happened all the same. [*To his father*] So brace yourself: the next offensive will be launched by the young.

GRAVEL: Against the old, I take it?

ANDRÉ: Yes! It's all over, that revolting little game where the beds of war and politics are never made by the young suckers who sleep in them.

GRAVEL: It'd be worth seeing, this Quebec kindergarten of yours, built to order by babies still in diapers!

ANDRÉ, *to* NICOLE, *perhaps*: Not so long ago it was the parents who chose, according to their own greed and vanity, the dumb heiress their weak-kneed son would marry. . . . By now, we've made some progress: in private affairs a young person is allowed to plan his life without too much interference. But in public affairs, my boy, you get a hiding if you refuse to shack up for the rest of your days with the fat mare with eyes crossed coast to coast who was picked for you without your say-so by Daddy Pearson! The bride we spend our political future with, thank you, we'll choose ourselves—and it'll be in keeping with our age, not yours, you can be damn sure!

GRAVEL: You're making great sense, all right! "Watch, beloved countrymen, the boxing match is on: a battle royal, to the finish, between the fathers and sons of French Canada! Experience, Logic and Reason versus Recklessness, Conceit and Ignorance —in their natural state: that is, unpolluted by par-

ents. To be won once and for all, the Garden of Eden
in your backyard, bananas off the trees in January
and old-age pensions when you get out of college!"
[*To* LOUISE] To hear eyewash like that from your
own son, when you've surmounted handicaps that
he and the other young sheikhs of his age'll never
know! I jumped into life right in the middle of the
Depression. Instead of hanging around with my
pockets full of my father's money, waiting for the
right moment to slap him down, I had to work nights
washing dishes at the Northeastern Lunch to pay my
school fees. Just avoiding starvation was considered
a lucky break. If a man can be judged by the trials
he's taken in stride, then you're no match for
us, my smug young friends, when it comes to the
survival of the fittest!

ANDRÉ: Sure, you're respectable. You were born in
winter, deep in the national woods—the deepest.
The simple fact you've come out alive is a triumph
in itself.

GRAVEL: Start putting your ten fingers to work for you,
and let your idle brain get busy, before you cry
"Crap!" and flush us down the drain! Then you
might have a right to claim our generation is blocking
the glorious destiny of a mixed-up bunch of spoiled
brats!

ANDRÉ: Unhappily for you and for us, the challenge
you had to face makes it impossible for you—no
matter how willing—to understand the challenge we
have to face.

GRAVEL: That's right! Spring has sprung: the air is
warm, life is easy. Fade away, old men, we don't
need your mitts and snowshoes any more!

ANDRÉ: It's not your fault, but you grew up in a
colonial world, where submission to the English and

licking their boots were taught you as national virtues. Your most inspiring motto? "Endure to endure!" You sat blissfully on your rear ends at the side of the road, watching the English parade by, minting money and swelling with power, and you smiled approval like dear little friars under a vow of eternal poverty. And now you'd like to apply your system to our national heritage?

GRAVEL: Yes, but today all that's being changed!

ANDRÉ: You've always been ordered around, so now you're obsessed with the notion you could never stand on your own two feet. If Ottawa lets go your hand, bingo!—you're convinced you'll forever fall down and go boom. Know what you've got? The complex of the dog on the leash, who'll never go farther than his lousy doghouse, even if the leash is removed and he's whipped. How can you lead us to freedom? It's got you as scared as the plague and VD combined.

GRAVEL: Bull!

ANDRÉ: You complain that today's youth is quitting on you? Then where do we find the blind faith that could draw us after in your inspiring footsteps? Among your compromisers? your maybe-things-are-all-for-the-best gents? your healers of a dying Confederation? your political boxers with their hands tied by party strings?

GRAVEL: Stop piling it up: I get the drift. According to you, Ottawa must be the Sodom and Gomorrah of Canadian politics: not a single honest man—all traitors, thieves and imbeciles! Trash for the fires of the Separatist heaven! Who do you think you're fooling with these fables?

LOUISE: André, you exaggerate, with all the passion and intolerance of your age. The right, the truth, are

61

never wholly on one side. Life is going to teach you some hard lessons if you won't admit that.

ANDRÉ: I've never doubted it.

LOUISE: Whatever you may think, there are men there of integrity and ability, as dedicated as you are to our people.

GRAVEL: Granted, French Canada has a whole litany of grievances. I've admitted that in my speech for tomorrow, as bluntly and bitterly as you might. But good God, if we want to defend our rights let's stop barricading ourselves in the cellars of the Chateau de Ramezay and draw swords where the battle rages.

ANDRÉ: No government in Ottawa can grant Quebec half its demands without automatically demolishing itself.

GRAVEL: What do you know about it?

ANDRÉ: Your own party is up to its neck in the dilemma: either bow to Belle Quebec and lose the nine Ugly Sisters on the deal, or get tough with her to please the rest of the country, and so lose power, Quebec, and all. If you won't accept evidence as clear as that, then you're the visionary, the spinner of dreams.

GRAVEL: Your delicate sophistries might have carried weight three years ago, or even last year. But while you were plotting your little revolution, I'll have you know, the problem was daily being resolved upward without the inestimable advantage of your brilliant co-operation.

ANDRÉ: Oh yes: the way cancer gets cured by morphine.

GRAVEL *to* LOUISE: And now his dud fireworks are ready for lighting, he'll try on any caper, any paradox, to justify what he's doing.

LOUISE: André, no matter what you've said—and I've

learned a good deal from it—I still think your father's right when he says that by different means he'd achieve there the same ends you're after here.

ANDRÉ: No, Mother: it would be a waste of an honest man's good life, trying to work out a compromise with English Canada. He'd let loose with an occasional outburst in French, just to scare them, followed by a curtsy in English to show them there are no hard feelings. And he'd burst with pride, every third session or so, at getting through some itty-bit reform that'd keep Quebec from screaming too loud but wouldn't upset the Liberals in Ontario, in Newfoundland, in Alberta . . . and other beauty spots in the land of our fathers.

GRAVEL: You don't know what you're saying!

ANDRÉ: Itty-bit reforms you'd get, naturally—along with a slap on the back and broad smiles by the dozen! "Sure, Peter, but what does Quebec really want, after all? Be a good boy and state it over again, will you? No, we don't get you. Why don't you try spelling it backwards for a change? But don't worry, Peter: believe it or not, we have big plans for you. The time is coming damn fast when we'll be ready to kick you right in the ass! Another thirty years or so. What with immigration and the Pill, authoritative sociologists tell us that by the end of the century the damn Pea-Soupers won't represent more than seventeen per cent of the population. And then, chums, you can yell your heads off: we won't care a hoot. In back of the backwoods, that's where you'll find the French identity, and it can stay there till Doomsday!"

GRAVEL, *to* LOUISE, *exasperated*: How can you answer rubbish like that? You have a go at him: I'm fed to the teeth.

63

LOUISE: André, the odds are not fair. You dreaded this confrontation, so you've been steeling yourself for it for a long time. But it's hit us like a thunderclap and we're stunned. So it's easy for you to outmanœuvre us. I can't find anything to say to you, either. But I know that all the words I wish I could think of now to hold you back, words I can't find in my poor empty head, will come back to plague me weeks and months later . . . when it's too late, when I spend my nights picturing you on your cot: you, a wild bird, caged, stifled, paralyzed behind bars! [*After a sob which* NICOLE *cannot quite restrain*] Oh yes, Nicole my dear, we're bewitched by the pride men have, but it's hard to live with. [*To the other two*] My darlings, I don't know any more which of you is the least unreasonable. Only one thing I'm sure of: the winner of this trial, whoever he is, will come out of it as pitiful as the loser.

ANDRÉ: Perhaps more.

LOUISE: André, you're the only one who could still call a halt. . . .

ANDRÉ, *achingly*:   I can't.

LOUISE: You are headed straight for calamity with your fists clenched. Are you sure you've considered how ugly it can be?

ANDRÉ: Where I'm headed I've tried to figure out at least a dozen times. But I know the real thing will be worse than the worst I've imagined.

GRAVEL: Yes, my boy! You're above fear! You don't care about the hard knocks, you don't give a damn about your father or anyone . . . but in all charity I warn you: you're going to find playing at revolution an expensive hobby. Expect the sacred flame to get a shower bath.

ANDRÉ: I'm under no illusions, believe me.

GRAVEL: You'd better not be. Remember one thing
   above all: you're going to throw yourselves into the
   arms of the police—one a night for fifteen days—
   hoping to gain public sympathy by ridiculing the
   forces of law and order. But just wait: you've no idea
   yet what a humiliated cop is like. He won't forgive
   you for making a fool of him. After two or three
   days, when they've got the picture, they'll use any
   means at their disposal to make someone squeal
   and bring the farce to an end.

ANDRÉ: I've foreseen that too.

GRAVEL: You're the leader, and the only one, according to you, who knows the whole gang; so be pre-
   pared, poor devil, to scream out before you pass out.

LOUISE, *in revulsion*:   Pierre . . . no . . .

NICOLE *goes upstage for a moment to hide her
emotion.*

GRAVEL, *as grieved in his own way as the two women:*
   What! You think I enjoy talking like that to my own
   son? Good God, this is no time for sugar-coating the
   pill! [*He withdraws, panting.*]

ANDRÉ: Don't try to frighten me, Dad. For days I've
   been scared out of my wits. [*Troubled*] It's not that
   I don't give a damn about the hard knocks, about
   prison and all the woes in store for me. I'm afraid
   all right. Or that I don't care about the loss of your
   friendship, or the harm I'm doing you, or the suffering I cause Mother, or Nicole's heartache. Away
   from all of you, I'll be so miserably unhappy I'll be
   tempted often to curse the demon that drove me
   there.

LOUISE: So much suffering . . . for such a dubious purpose, such a debatable one . . . it makes no sense, my child, it makes no sense.

ANDRÉ: If I were a soldier, if they put a gun in my hands, and made me risk my skin in some absurd war started, as always, by comfortable old men, anxious to vindicate their mistakes and hold onto their loot, even if you were sad to see me go, would you try to hold me back?

GRAVEL: And your own little war, which no one else is forcing you to start: you're certain-sure it's super-legitimate and sacrosanct? In your heart of hearts, all's bright and light?

ANDRÉ: No. I'm not absolutely certain I'm not making a mistake.

GRAVEL: You're in doubt about it? You admit it?

ANDRÉ: Yes.

GRAVEL *to* LOUISE: But his mind's irrevocably made up, all the same, to carry us all down together into his abyss!

LOUISE, *to* ANDRÉ: If you're not completely convinced, how can you take on such a frightening responsibility?

ANDRÉ: Need a priest prove to himself he's absolutely right to believe in God before he commits his life to Him? He may reason it out for years, but there'll come a time when he's got to rely on faith, and faith can't ever exclude doubt.

GRAVEL: Mister Toad ducks again! "It's a matter of faith . . . in the spirit of the saints, I argue no more." You're evading the issue! You've run out of your festering arguments, your back is against the wall, so you scurry like a rat into a hole.

ANDRÉ: No. I'm not evading anything. The biggest risk I'm taking hasn't got through to you yet—and you a lawyer! If fascination with your own wound'd let you be more objective, you'd have realized by now that the sentence I'll get will cut me off for life from the practice of law. Code of the Bar, Chapter Two, Article Forty-eight. [GRAVEL *reacts as if struck*.] The independence of Quebec will give me the only chance I'll ever get to return some day to my chosen profession. So you see, I'm not trying to cheat: I'm jumping without a net. If I miss the trapeze I've had it.

GRAVEL: Louise, it's utter madness!

ANDRÉ: Nicole, nothing, absolutely nothing, forces you to take the jump with me. On the contrary, everything points the other way if you decide I'm not the one you thought you loved. Better to cry for a while than make us both miserable by not facing up to it honestly and courageously.

GRAVEL, *to* ANDRÉ: That's an easy way to play the martyr, taking for granted that next month a revolution will be announced with a trumpet blast. . .

ANDRÉ: No . . .

GRAVEL: . . . and a delirious crowd'll sweep in, break your chains and switch your crime sheet to a national hero's diploma! But you're writing yourself a Batman serial, boy!

ANDRÉ: No, I know the battle will be long.

GRAVEL: You won't live to see the end of it. . . .

ANDRÉ: Long . . . and bitter enough for a man to cry quits.

GRAVEL: . . . Ever! The public will never go along!

ANDRÉ: But some day it'll have to come to an end. . .

GRAVEL: Who cares about independence when he's happy the way he is?

ANDRÉ: . . . even if you wait till the year two thousand.

GRAVEL: To them a new road or a raise in salary will always speak louder than principles.

ANDRÉ, *mainly for himself*: Whatever you want, let them prove you have no right to it. . .

GRAVEL: It's stupid, but that's the way it is!

ANDRÉ: . . . but if you have a right to it, don't let them tell you you can never have it.

GRAVEL: You're not going to change any of that!

ANDRÉ: Justice always wins in the end.

GRAVEL, *seeking a way to keep him*: There are things which are possible and things which are not!

ANDRÉ: It's a question of patience, that's all. . . .

GRAVEL: Say what you like and do as you please, you can't live without compromise.

ANDRÉ: . . . All the more reason not to give up.

GRAVEL, *pleading*: Don't waste your life crying out in the desert!

ANDRÉ, *stubbornly*: Give up, and you'll never find peace. . .

GRAVEL: You're nothing but a bunch of visionaries!

ANDRÉ: . . . you'll kick yourself as long as you live.

GRAVEL: Even those who're with you now will drop you, one by one. . .

ANDRÉ: Even if you were alone. . .

GRAVEL: . . . and tell you it's better to live in the real world after all!

ANDRÉ: Even if you were all alone, it wouldn't change a thing. . . .

NICOLE *comes and sits by him and takes his arm.*

GRAVEL, *sensing that* ANDRÉ *has eluded him*: You talked about Sweden a moment ago: the United States would never let us set up a socialist state right next door to them.

ANDRÉ: . . . That's why there's no point discussing it any further.

GRAVEL: With ten provinces we've all the trouble in

the world seeing they don't take over in every way conceivable.

ANDRÉ, *fed up*: There's no point!

GRAVEL: How do you expect Quebec to go it alone, lost in an ocean of two hundred million speaking English?

NICOLE, *champing at the bit*: He has no choice, can't you see? Sure it'd be easier for him to give in and live happily ever after, but he can't! It's not his fault: he can't do it! Everyone can't be born meek and mild and careful!

GRAVEL, *to* NICOLE: Listen—

NICOLE, *pouring out her heart*: If he's daring and a little crazy, good for him. It's a change! Since 1759, haven't we had it up to here with cowards, weaklings and sissies?

GRAVEL, *wanting to recapture control of the discussion*: Nicole, this is something for us to—

NICOLE, *a small fury*: Listen yourself! You've been jawing away long enough: now it's my turn. And if you don't want to hear what I have to say, cover your ears! It won't make any difference, 'cause you don't understand anything anyway. It's not surprising you two don't get along: you don't speak the same language! What he calls independence, an open window on the world, freedom to support Quebec's interests over Ontario's, you and the other alumni of the Faculty of British Sciences call narrow separatism, going back into a shell, collective suicide, a Chinese Wall around Quebec and a medieval ghetto!

GRAVEL: Catch his hay fever if you want: you'll soon get over it—you'll see!

NICOLE: Have you any idea what a colonial you are, even in your own home? [*Practically under his nose*] An hour ago, on the phone, you were talking to

69

your big boss, the Prime Minister of what you quiveringly call my beloved country. Had you felt the temptation, perfectly legitimate for a free man, to make him answer you in your mother tongue, can you imagine how bewildered the poor dear great man would've been? And yet three out of ten of "his people" speak French. And Confederation is hardly a surprise—it's been around for a century! What's more, a Nobel Prize winner isn't usually a dunce. So? He can't speak our language, or he won't speak it? Either way, you can kiss every finger of both his hands if you want to, but personally I say, "Nuts! Crap!" [*To* LOUISE] Forgive me, Mrs. Gravel, but it had to come out. And don't be too worried about André. His father was telling me before you came in —and it's the most intelligent thing he's said all night—that, before he proposed, André wanted to make sure I knew him through and through. Now I know everything, I wish I could coin a word even more loving to say I love him. I'll never be ashamed of him: anything but. Others can hang their heads at the mention of his name; now I'll lift mine up proudly and tell everyone who wants to know, "I am the fiancée of André Gravel, the political prisoner." And when he comes out, if he still wants me, body and soul and everything else, I'll be waiting for him at the door with my suitcase. I'll help him and protect him whenever he needs me: I may not look it, but I have a sturdy bumper. I was crying a while ago, but not any more. [*She throws her kleenex over her shoulder.*] And if anybody wants to give his sacred flame a shower bath I'll dry it out and light it up again: fire is what I've got enough for two of! If I don't die first I'll be at his side, for better or worse, till the end of his reign.

GRAVEL: His reign? Come off it!

NICOLE: Yes, his reign! Because when his trials are over he'll have triumphs instead. I'll put it in writing! The instant, ready-mix victory you were after is chicken feed compared with the one he'll win in the long run!

GRAVEL: My poor dear, you don't know what's in store for you!

NICOLE: Keep your pity: you're going to need it. And don't worry about me, I won't be pitiable. When I'm forty, I won't have to beg a psychiatrist to give me a reason for living: I'll have one. The Voice of Women, in my day, is going to be heard outside the delivery room! [*To* LOUISE] I'm not referring to you, Mrs. Gravel, because I admire you and I love you an awful lot for giving me a man like the one you raised, morally and physically. If my children are up to yours, that's all I ask. And I don't hold any of the things you said earlier against you: you're enough of a woman to know your place is at your husband's side, even if among his numerous qualities he's as old-fashioned and one-track-minded as a pre-war trolley-car! [*She falls back beside* ANDRÉ, *short of breath.*] Whew! I'm beat! [*To* ANDRÉ] Now, love, it breaks my heart to have to tell you, but when I looked at the clock five minutes ago it was ten to nine.

ANDRÉ, *waking up*: Yes: that's right. I must go. [*He gets up painfully.*]

GRAVEL, *going to him*: No, André . . . don't go.

ANDRÉ: Please . . . let me by.

GRAVEL, *begging*: Today, you're the stronger: don't take advantage of it. I'll be grateful as long as I live.

ANDRÉ: It's too late. . . .

71

The clock begins to sound nine.

GRAVEL: If I've wronged you in any way, I humbly ask your forgiveness.

ANDRÉ: It's too late. I've got to go.

GRAVEL, *panic-stricken*:   I'm not asking for myself. Give this up and I'll never touch politics again, not with a ten-foot pole, I swear.

ANDRÉ: It's out of my hands now. . . .

GRAVEL: Don't go! You said, didn't you, that someone else could take your place?

ANDRÉ: It wouldn't make any difference.

GRAVEL: You'll explain to them what happened: they'll understand.

ANDRÉ: If I let my replacement do it, it wouldn't make any difference: don't you see?

GRAVEL, *gripping* ANDRÉ *by the lapels*:   André, André! You can't do this to me! [*He slaps him.*] My favourite son, my pal. . .

ANDRÉ, *putting up no defence and almost crying himself*: It wouldn't prevent the scandal. . . .

GRAVEL, *continuing to strike him*:   My pal . . . the apple of my eye!

ANDRÉ: Don't you get it? My replacement is—[*Another slap cuts off the sentence.*]

LOUISE, *a cry*:   It's Larry!

ANDRÉ: Yes, it's him.

GRAVEL, *letting him go, stunned*:   What?

ANDRÉ: It's Larry! Yes, I tell you it's Larry!

SCENE EIGHT

O'BRIEN *enters from the outside.*

O'BRIEN, *without troubling to doff his coat*:   In the

72

cab, I just heard that the monument to Edward VII,
in Wolseley Park, went down three minutes ago.

LOUISE, *to* O'BRIEN: Larry . . . where is he?

O'BRIEN: He left me at the Windsor. I thought he'd be
here.

LOUISE, *faced with the evidence*:   Oh my God, it's him!

O'BRIEN: Who? [*Coming to* ANDRÉ] Your replacement?

The telephone rings.

O'BRIEN, *answering, since he is closest to the phone*:
Yes? . . . Where are you, Larry? . . . Just a minute.
[*To* ANDRÉ] He wants to speak to you.

LOUISE, *to* O'BRIEN: Where is he?

O'BRIEN: At my place.

ANDRÉ, *on the phone*:   Why so early? It wasn't time
yet. . .

O'BRIEN, *after consulting his watch, he taps* ANDRÉ *on
the shoulder*:   It's now nine-thirty. [*Ill at ease*]
Before I left, a while ago, I put back the clock.

ANDRÉ, *on the phone*:   Okay, Larry: I didn't know. . .
Nobody saw you? . . . Don't move from there, you
hear? [*Despite his exhaustion, he is once more the
leader*.] As agreed, I go to the police. . . . Don't
argue: that's an order. . . . [*Gently, before hanging
up*] Larry . . . thanks, kid.

LOUISE: André . . . why did you choose . . . him?

ANDRÉ: He had to do his share. I thought I'd found a
good way of keeping him at arm's length. [*To*
O'BRIEN] Thanks to you, I failed.

O'BRIEN: May I go with you?

ANDRÉ: No. Look after Larry, right away. Keep him
from doing anything foolish. That's all I ask.

O'BRIEN *goes out.*

ANDRÉ: I'll get my things ready.

He goes up to his room. NICOLE, *after a moment's hesitation, goes after him and takes him by the arm.*

GRAVEL, *crushed, after a silence*:   Louise . . .
LOUISE, *through her own sorrow*:   Yes, dear?
GRAVEL: Louise . . . what's happening to us?
LOUISE: Yesterday, they were children dancing in the house. . . . Today they've become men . . . ready to fight in the street.
GRAVEL: Against us?
LOUISE: Against their fate.
GRAVEL: They had everything to make them happy.
LOUISE: Others, perhaps . . . not them.
GRAVEL, *lost*:   What's to be done now?
LOUISE: Refuse what isn't yours to accept, any more. But give that talk of yours tomorrow.
GRAVEL: I wouldn't have the strength.
LOUISE: You've got to find it. To make their way, your sons have pushed you into the ditch. But you can't stay there. Their right to assert themselves as men doesn't rob you of the right to continue on your way. If your convictions haven't changed . . .
GRAVEL: Their solution isn't the right one, that I know!
LOUISE: Then you don't have a choice either. Your duty is clear. Don't be afraid: those who hear you tomorrow will not despise you. Courage always commands respect. [GRAVEL *gets up with an effort*.] You can tell them truths which more than ever they'll have an obligation to understand.

The doorbell rings, and the SECRETARY *appears discreetly in the hallway.*

74

SECRETARY, *greeting* LOUISE: Evening, Mrs. Gravel. [*To* GRAVEL, *putting her evening's work down*] Well, it's all copied.

GRAVEL: Thank you.

SECRETARY: Except the ending. If you've got it, I could take it down now.

GRAVEL: Would you?

SECRETARY: I'd be delighted to. [*She has already removed her coat and sits, ready to take dictation.*] By the way, your reservation has been confirmed for the ten-thirty plane.

GRAVEL, *dictating*: Gentlemen . . . by now, you all know that my own house is divided over the problem that—together—we have faced today.

ANDRÉ, *a small suitcase in his hand, comes down the stairs after* NICOLE. *During the following speech, he goes to his mother and embraces her.*

GRAVEL, *still dictating*: I know that you share my distress. . . .

LOUISE, *holding* ANDRÉ *by the hand as he starts to go*: Pierre . . . I think your son would like to shake hands with you.

ANDRÉ *lowers his head. After a short moment of hesitation, he goes slowly to his father. In silence, scarcely looking at one another, they shake hands. Then* ANDRÉ *goes upstage, where he stands a moment, lost.*

GRAVEL, *picking up his dictation*: I know that you share my distress, and that of my wife. . . .

NICOLE, *after waiting in the hallway, she has come to get*

the bag which ANDRÉ *left on a chair when he came to embrace his mother*: Let's go. [*She takes* ANDRÉ *by the arm.*]

During the following speech, LOUISE, *sitting near her husband, watches the young couple disappear out the door.*

GRAVEL, *dictating*: . . . For my divided house will not go down without shaking yours to its very foundations.

The curtain falls.